JUST ADD KIDS

Downright Upright

and 50 Other
Bible Games for
Elementary
Children

Abingdon Press
Nashville

Just Add Kids: Downright Upright and 50 Other Bible Games for Elementary Children

ISBN 0-687-04890-7

Lead Editor: Daphna Flegal
Editor: Betsi H. Smith
Contributing Writers: LeeDell Stickler, Judy Newman-St. John, Marcia Stoner
Designed by: Paige Easter
Illustrated by: Megan Jeffery (page 85: Jim Padgett)
Cover Photographs: Ron Benedict

03 04 05 06 07 08 09—10 9 8 7 6 5 4 3 2

MANUFACTURED IN THE UNITED STATES OF AMERICA

ELEmentary Games
Table of Contents

4

Introduction
Welcome to Just Add Kids

As you look out across your classroom, you see one child yawning, another child trying to climb a bookshelf, and two others in a shoving match. What will you do with them? Maybe it's time to play a game.

Downright Upright and 50 Other Bible Games for Elementary Children is loaded with games that will cure your classroom blahs. Some use reproducible pages, which are included here. And since each game in *Downright Upright* relates to a specific event in the Bible, your children are learning while they're playing.

Each child in your class is unique, with his or her own family background and experiences. But elementary children do have some common traits. Understanding those traits will help you in your classroom:

- They are restless and energetic, and would rather participate than watch or listen. Each one of them is growing at a different rate.
- They are concrete thinkers, but they are just beginning to develop an ability to reason and discuss. They are curious and have great imaginations.
- They are becoming less dependent on parents. They enjoy playing with other children, but will often imitate adults in their actions.

For guidelines on how to make the most out of your game time, see the article on the next page. For other resources that will help you make your class time the best that it can be, don't miss the other books in the *Just Add Kids* collection:

- *The Jailhouse Rocked and 50 Other Bible Stories for Elementary Children.*
- *From Bags to Bushes and 50 Other Bible Crafts for Elementary Children.*
- *Don't Get Wet Feet and 50 Other Bible Stories for Preschoolers.*
- *Ring 'Round Jericho and 50 Other Bible Games for Preschoolers.*
- *Footprints on the Wall and 50 Other Bible Crafts for Preschoolers.*

Using Games to Teach God's Word

Children learn through movement. As they hop, stretch, race, and parade, they are grasping the principles that each particular game is designed to teach. Games also provide a welcome break from the classroom routine. They give children a chance to fellowship and to have fun together. And for those children who don't excel at reading or crafts, game time may be the only time some children feel they are doing something well.

Follow these simple guidelines to make game time fun, safe, and successful.

- **Plan ahead.** Decide where the game will be played in your classroom, and clear the space ahead of time. Make any signs, props, or game cards you will be using. Practice the game yourself, to make sure you understand exactly how it should be played.

- **Balance activities.** Choose where game time will fall in your lesson plan. You might not want to play an active game just before you want the children to sit quietly for your worship time. But games can work well after the children have been sitting for a while.

- **Put safety first.** Clear the area of hazards. Check for slippery floors; if you've just finished a messy craft, look for spills on the floor. Remove any rugs that can move or trip a child. Move furniture out of the way. Make sure there are no sharp edges on tables or counter tops. If the game involves a ball, caution the children to never throw a ball at someone's face.

- **Be aware of disabilities.** If a child in your classroom has a physical or mental disability, use games that will let that child participate on an equal footing with the others. If the child has a mobility problem, avoid or adapt games that involve running. If the child has a learning disability, avoid or adapt games that involve putting letters in order.

- **Play cooperatively.** Whenever possible, remove the element of competition from the games you play. Encourage the children to clap for everyone. Find something positive to say about each child, not just the fastest or the smartest. If you are giving out prizes, give them to everyone. Say, for example: "You all played the game so well, I want everyone to have a sticker." Having fun should be more important than winning.

Creation of Animals

Game 1

Supplies: habitat sheet (see page 10), scissors

Guess the Homes

Prior to class, make a copy of the habitat sheet (see page 10). Cut the six habitat areas apart and place one on each table.

Assign each child to a table. (Each table should have at least two children.)

Say: Each table has a special habitat where many different kinds of animals can live. Each team will choose one animal that it believes lives there. Don't tell the other teams. The other teams will try to guess what that animal is. Don't tell the other teams. They can ask questions that can be answered with a yes or a no.

The team that guesses correctly gets a point. When all the habitats are presented, the team with the most points wins.

Say: In God's creation every creature has a special place to belong. Every animal has a home. God intended for every person to have a home. But what about God? Where does God live? (*Most children will say that God lives at church.*)

Ask: What do we call God's house? What do we do in God's house? Is this the only place that God lives? (*No, God is everywhere.*)

Bible
Genesis
1:20-25

Game 2

Animal Charades

Say: Each plant and each animal has a special place in God's creation. Sometimes we do not understand the purpose behind some of God's creatures. For example, who really needs a mosquito?

Let the children answer. If necessary, point out that mosquitoes breed on water, where they are eaten by fish. Herons in turn eat the fish, so that makes mosquitoes an important part of the food chain.

Say: To assume that an animal has no place in God's plan is to be short-sighted. It is our responsibility as Christians to care for God's creatures. Think how sad God must be when an animal becomes extinct.

Ask: What is your favorite animal?

Let the children share their responses.

Say: Let's act them out. One at a time you will act out a favorite animal or an animal you think is really neat. Let's see if the rest of the class can guess what it is.

Let each child come to the front and, one at a time, imitate the animal that he or she chose. If you have time, you might want to categorize the animals. Let the children act out their favorite birds, sea creatures, and land creatures.

Expect to get some dinosaurs. They too were a part of God's creation.

10

In God's Image

Game 1

Category Chaos

Ask: When you look around, you can see that each of us, no matter how different, has some things in common. What are they? (*two legs, two eyes, a nose, two ears, and so forth*). (Be sensitive to any children in your class who may have a disability of some sort.)

Say: Even though God created each of us different in many ways, we are also alike in many others. I am going to call out several categories. I want you to group yourselves together according to similarities. For example, if I say eye color, then everyone will try to find other people who have the same eye color. If I say hair color, the group will do the same thing. If you cannot find someone who matches you, you become a group of one.

Add the categories of gender and favorite foods.

Say: It's easy to forget when we are celebrating our differences that we have many things in common.

Game 2

Let's Reflect

Divide the children into pairs. One child will be the leader, and the other will be the mirror. The mirror will try to do everything the leader does as the leader is doing it.

Say: Today we are going to talk about the creation of human beings. The Bible says that human beings are created in the image of God.

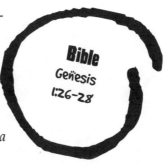

Bible
Genesis
1:26-28

Ask: What is an image? (*a likeness of something that closely resembles the original*) Where might you see an image? (*in something that reflects, like a*

mirror) What do mirrors tell us? (*what we look like*) If we are created in the image of God, does that mean we all look like God? (*No; but we are created to resemble God in our actions and in our choices.*)

Game 3

Glue Tag

Bring the children together in an open area. Select one child to be IT.

Say: The object of this game is for IT to gather everyone up into one group. Whenever IT touches you, you must hold onto ITs waist and go everywhere that IT goes. Then IT and the person who was tagged become IT and go after someone else. When that person is tagged, he or she goes to the end of the line and holds onto the last person's waist.

When the whole group is a part of the line, the game is over. As the line gets longer, the persons who are a part of the line cannot let go, but they can help IT capture the last remaining persons by blocking their paths or by surrounding them.

Give the children a few minutes to see how long it takes for IT to gather all the children into the line. If the children enjoy the game, select another IT and play again.

Say: The game wasn't over until everyone was included in the line. In today's Bible lesson we learn how we are all a part of God's plan for creation, every one of us.

12

The Garden of Eden

Game 1

Supplies: newspaper, tall kitchen garbage bags, masking tape

Partner Pickup

Divide the children into pairs. Let each pair of children take newspaper, crumple it, and stuff it into a tall kitchen garbage bag. When the bag is sufficiently stuffed, tie it off and tape it so that it doesn't come undone.

Make a starting line on one side of the room and a pickup line on the opposite side of the room. Place all the garbage bags on the pickup line.

Say: Everyone knows that working together makes a job easier. Let's play a game of partners. The two partners will really have to rely on each other.

Have the partners stand side by side with inside arms either linked or about each other's waists. Use the plastic grocery bags to tie the partners' inside legs together.

The object of the game is for the partners to cross the room, pick up their garbage bag, and come back across the line. The partner on the right can only use his or her right hand. The partner on the left can only use his or her left hand.

Let the children practice moving together. Then have them line up on the start line. Say "go" and let each pair of children hobble across the room and retrieve their garbage bag.

When everyone has returned to the start, let the children untie their legs, sit down, and talk about the experience.

Ask: What did you have to do in this game? (*You had to work together*.) Was it easy? Was it more fun? (*yes*)

Say: The Bible tells us the story about the first man and the first woman and a very special garden called Eden. It was in this special garden that God placed Adam and Eve. At first Adam was all alone, but this didn't last forever.

Bible
Genesis
2:7-23

Game 2

Supplies: small ball

It's Lonely Here

Have the children form a circle in the center of the room. Select one child to begin the game. IT will be the first human being.

Say: When God created the first human being, that person was all alone. He had no one to talk to, and no one to help him tend the beautiful garden that God had given to him. So God decided to create a partner for him. Today, IT is going to be the very first human being. IT is terribly lonely. Look lonely, IT! IT needs to select a partner.

IT will walk around the outside of the circle. The rest of the children will stand in the circle with their hands behind their backs. Make sure their hands are open enough for IT to place the ball in them.

As IT walks around the circle, IT says: "It's very lonely here. I need a partner. I wonder who it'll be." As IT goes around the outside of the circle, IT will place the ball in someone's hand. The person who has the ball will chase IT.

If IT gets back to that person's space before IT has been tagged, then the person with the ball becomes the next IT. If the person with the ball gets back to his or her space first, IT must try again with another person.

© 1999 Abingdon Press.

14

Noah

Game 1

Supplies: animal cards (see page 17), blue crepe paper, tape, scissors, box or basket

What Am I?

Before the children arrive, cut six-foot strips of blue crepe paper and hang them in the doorway to simulate rain or water.

Photocopy the animal cards (see page 17), making sure you have enough animals for each child to have one. Cut them apart and put them in a box or basket face down so they are convenient as the children arrive, but not visible.

Greet the children warmly as they come in. Without letting them see the animal, attach an animal card to their backs with masking tape.

> **Say:** What I am putting on your back is part of a game we will be playing when everyone arrives. Don't peek or ask your friends what is on your back. You are to discover what animal is on your back. You cannot look in a mirror. You cannot ask a friend to tell you. What you can do is ask one or more friends questions that can be answered by a "yes" or a "no." For example, does the animal have legs? Does the animal have fur? When you think you have the identity of the animal on your back, come and whisper your guess to me. If you are right, then you can move the animal card from your back to your front. If you are wrong, you must keep asking questions.

Children who have a difficult time may be given strategic hints. As the children discover their animals, make sure the animals are taped securely to their front.

> **Ask:** What Bible story do you know that has animals in it—a big boat, and a great flood?

> **Say:** That's right, the story of Noah. And from the story of Noah, we learn something very important about God.

Bible
Genesis 6:14–7:17;
8:6–19; 9:13

15

Game 2

Supplies: chairs, cards from previous activity (see page 17)

In the Ark

Have the children bring their chairs into a circle. Leave the middle large and open. Select one child to be Noah. Remove that child's chair from the circle. If you have done the previous activity, "What Am I?" (see page 15), have each child continue wearing the same animal card. If you did not play "What Am I?" photocopy the cards from page 17. Cut them apart and tape one to each child.

Say: Noah stands in the middle and calls out the name of an animal. It must be one of the animals in our circle. Noah names one animal at a time. The child (or children) with that animal card must go into the "ark" (*Gesture to the center of the circle.*) beside Noah. At a certain point, Noah will call, "Everyone out!" All the animals that are in the center of the circle must find a new seat. Noah tries to get one of the empty seats.

The person left without a seat becomes Noah. Noah may call to the ark as many or as few animals as he or she chooses before saying, "Everyone out!" Noah may also call out, "Ark aground!" Then all the animals have to change places, and once again Noah tries to find a place.

© 1997 Abingdon Press.

17

Towel of Babel

Game

Supplies: women's high-heeled shoes, men's boots, index cards, toothpicks and modeling clay

Tower Power

Ask everyone to remove his or her shoes and pile them in the middle of the floor. If possible, add a pair of women's high-heeled shoes and a pair of men's boots to the pile.

Divide the students into three teams.

   Say: In this game each team will build a special tower.

Ask one team to build a tower using the shoes. Ask the second team to build a tower using index cards. Ask the third team to build a tower using only two colors of modeling clay and toothpicks. (Ask the team members not to combine the colors of the clay.)

Give the students six minutes to work.

   Ask: What was hard about building your tower? What were you thinking while you were working? What were you hoping your tower would be like?

   Say: The Bible tells us about a tower that the people built high in the sky. They wanted their tower to go all the way to heaven. We will find out what happened to the people who built the tower.

Bible
Genesis
11:1–9

Abraham and Sarah

Game 1

Supplies: two suitcases or large briefcases filled with old clothes, a pair of shoes, a hat, a purse, and so forth

Ready to Move

Gather the children in an open area. Divide the children into two teams.

Ask: What is the first thing you do when you are moving? (*Pack up all your belongings*.) Today we are going to play a packing game.

Fill two suitcases or large briefcases with old clothes, a pair of shoes, a hat, a purse, and so forth. Give one suitcase to the leader of each team. The first person on each team must carry the suitcase to the finish line, open it, dump out the contents, put on a clothing item or shoes, take it off again, pick up everything, repack, close the suitcase, and run back to the starting line. The game will continue until all members of one team have finished.

Say: God gave God's people their start a long time ago. One person trusted God and continued to trust God, even though everything seemed impossible. We can learn to trust God from such people of faith.

Game 2

Supplies: masking tape, variety of objects for obstacle course, blindfold

Trust Me

Bring the children together in the open space of your classroom. Mark a square of about ten feet by ten feet along one side of the classroom with masking tape.

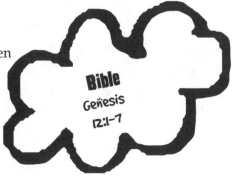

Bible
Genesis
12:1–7

Have the children stand around the square.

Ask: Do you think you can walk across the square? (*Have the children one at a time walk across the square.*) Could you do it blindfolded? (*Yes, but it would be a little more difficult.*) Could you do it blindfolded without stepping on anything?

Scatter a variety of objects around the square so that the children would have difficulty navigating the space without direction.

Say: We are going to play a game called "Who Do You Trust?" Each of you will in turn be blindfolded and will walk from one side of the square to the other. You will select one person that you trust to give you verbal directions before you begin. (*Directions should be simple, such as "two steps forward," "one side step to the right," "one side step to the left," "giant step forward," and so forth.*)

Ask: Do you think that this game was a little like what Abraham and Sarah had to do when they packed up everything? God invites us to be a part of God's family today. But like Abraham and Sarah we have to trust God and know that God will guide us, just as Abraham and Sarah trusted God long ago.

Game 3

Supplies: masking tape, newspaper

Grassy Grazing

Create two fields for the sheep to graze in, using masking tape. Make sure there is space between. Give each child a small stack of newspapers. Have the children crumple the newspaper pages into balls and scatter them in the two fields.

Say: You are my flock of sheep. The newspaper is the grass you eat every day. I have brought you to the meadow to graze. (*Point to the first area of the room.*) I want you to go grazing. (*Have the children pick up the crumpled newspaper balls.*) Come and stand next to me when all the grass is gone. (*Point to the second field when the first field is cleared.*) All right, let's move on to the next field.

Say: Today we are going to learn about the early settlers of the Holy Land. They were nomads, which meant they moved around a lot because their flocks needed food. Their homes had to move with them.

Jacob and Esau

Game

Supplies: lunch-size paper bags, rubber bands, marker, large sheet of paper, tape or tacks; grapes, marbles, modeling clay, balloons (not inflated), sponge shapes

Hands Only Game

Before the children arrive, place one of the items listed above in the supplies list inside each paper bag. (You may add items of your own.) Put a rubber band around the top of each sack so that the children cannot see inside the bag. Write a letter or number on the outside of the bag. Set the bags around the room.

Create a grid on the wall with a box for each bag. As the children move about the room, they will write on the grid what they think is in the bag. (If you have non-readers, have a teacher stand at the grid and write each child's suggestions.)

As the children arrive, greet them warmly and get them started.

Say: As we wait for everyone to get here, I want you to try to solve a mystery. Each bag has something in it. You will go around the room and try to discover what is in each bag. The only catch is that all you can do is feel it. When you think you know, go over to the chart and record your guess.

When everyone has had a chance to feel the insides of each bag, bring the children to the circle. Go over the chart. Then take the contents out and show them to the children.

Ask: Which was the hardest to identify? the easiest?

Say: The Bible tells a story about a young man who is able to fool his father because his father is blind. But even though what he does is wrong, he soon discovers an important fact.

Bible
Genesis
27:1–29

Jacob's Dream

Game 1

Supplies: construction paper, scissors, masking tape

Rock Tag

Cut pieces of construction paper into irregular shapes that will resemble rocks. Make sure there is one rock for each child, minus one. Scatter the rocks about the room. Secure the rocks to the floor with a loop of masking tape.

Say: Today we're talking about Jacob, who used a rock for a pillow. After his dream he took this rock, stood it up, and poured oil over it. Jacob knew that he had done wrong. But the rock became a symbol that God still cared about him and would bring him safely back to his homeland again.

Say: Let's play a game. In our game the only safe places in the room are the rocks. A child who is moving between rocks can be tagged. A child who is standing on a rock is safe.

Select one child to be IT. If IT tags a child who is moving between rocks, then the two exchange places. No one can stand on a rock for more than ten seconds (a slow count to ten).

Two children may not occupy the same rock. If a person comes to a rock, then the person who was there must leave.

Play the game until several children have an opportunity to be IT. Remind the children that this rock reminded Jacob that God's love is always with him.

Bible
Genesis
28:10-22

Game 2

Me and My Shadow

Say: One of you is the person; the other is the shadow. Shadows have to go and move everywhere their person goes and moves. Talk among yourselves and decide who will be the person and who will be the shadow. When I blow the whistle, you will reverse roles. I will tell the person what to do and how to move. The shadow must follow as close behind as possible.

Call out movements such as these:

Everyone walk.
Everyone walk very fast.
Everyone hop.
Everyone jump.
Everyone skip.
Everyone tiptoe.
Everyone crawl.

Let the children move about the room. Blow the whistle several times so that the children get to be both person and shadow. Then bring the children together in the circle.

Ask: Was it fun to have someone so close to you, doing everything that you do? Did you know that there is someone who is even closer than that to you? Who do you think it is? (*God*)

Say: That's right. God is always with us, even closer than a shadow. God knows what we think. God knows what we feel. God knows us like no one else. God is always there for us.

Joseph and His Brothers

Game 1

Supplies: spring-type clothespins, chairs, blankets or sheets

Clothespin Tag

Attach a clothespin to the back of each child's shirt or dress. Designate an area of the classroom to be the pit by putting chairs in a circle, the seats facing out. Make sure there is enough space for each child to sit in the pit, with his or her legs extended. Take several blankets or sheets and throw over the backs of the chairs, enclosing the circle.

Say: Each of you has one clothespin, but you want more. You don't just want your own; you want the ones that belong to the rest of the group. The object is for you to try to get the clothespin of someone else without someone getting yours. When your clothespin is gone, then you must go into the pit.

Play music as the children try to get one another's clothespins. When most of the children are in the pit, call the game.

Ask: How does it feel in the pit? scary? exciting? Today we're talking about a Bible character who probably had those feelings. And how he got there was something terrible that his brothers did to him.

© 1998 Abingdon Press.

Game 2

Supplies: trade items (see page 26), scissors, envelopes, basket or box, ball

Jealousy

Photocopy and cut apart the trade items (see page 26). Put one in each envelope. If you have more than eight children in class, make two copies of the items, but leave out the second "Gotcha" card. Place the envelopes in a basket or box or spread them out on a table. Bring the children together in a circle.

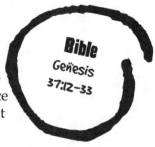

Bible
Genesis
37:12–33

24

Ask: Has a friend or family member ever gotten something really special? Did you ever wish you had gotten something like it, or even better? The object of this game is to get the important prize without getting the GOTCHA card. Each of you will have a choice, except for the first person. You either can get your own envelope or trade with someone who already has a prize. Do you want what your neighbor's got, or do you want to take a chance?

Toss the ball to one of the children. That person will go first. When he or she opens the envelope, have him or her hold up the picture. Everyone will cheer. Then throw the ball to another child.

Ask: (*Name*), do you want what Shari's got, (*name the item*), or do you want to take a chance on getting something better?

Play until someone gets the GOTCHA card.

Say: The Bible tells a story about a time when jealousy caused trouble in a family. God doesn't want us to be jealous of one another. God wants us to love one another.

Game 3

Parrot Talk

Have the children sit in a circle facing the teacher.

Say: I am going to say a sentence about the Bible story of Joseph and his brothers. If it is true, then you will repeat it back to me. If it isn't true, then you will put your hand over your mouth.

Use these sentences:

Joseph had many brothers.
Joseph's brothers loved him very much.
Joseph had a special coat.
Each of Joseph's brothers had a coat like his.
Joseph had special dreams.
Joseph's dreams were about being President.
Joseph's brothers didn't like Joseph's dreams.
Joseph was a tattletale.
Jacob sent Joseph to the grocery store.
Jacob sent Joseph out to find his brothers.
His brothers greeted him with hugs.
His brothers ambushed him and threw him in a pit.
The brothers sold Joseph to an amusement park.
The brothers sold Joseph to traders.
The brothers threw Joseph's coat away.
The brothers dipped his coat in goat's blood.
Jacob was very sad.

Baby Moses

Game

Supplies: baby (see page 28), scissors, tape

Hide the Baby

Before class, assemble the reed basket and baby Moses (see page 28). Roll baby Moses into a tube shape and secure with tape. Fold the sides of the basket together into a box shape. Place the baby in the basket and secure the lid.

Say: Today we are going to pretend that we are the princess who has come to the river to take a bath. She hears a baby crying and is trying to find it.

Select one child to be IT. IT will close his or her eyes as the teacher hides the baby (see page 28). When baby Moses is hidden, let IT open his or her eyes.

The object is for IT to find baby Moses using the hints the class provides. The class provides the hints by crying like a baby. The closer IT comes to the baby, the louder the class members cry. The farther away IT moves from the baby, the softer the class members cry.

When IT finds the baby, then IT selects the next child to be IT.

Say: Baby Moses' family loved and cared for him. They kept him safe from the king. Let's name some ways that we can show love to our family.

Bible
Exodus
2:1-10

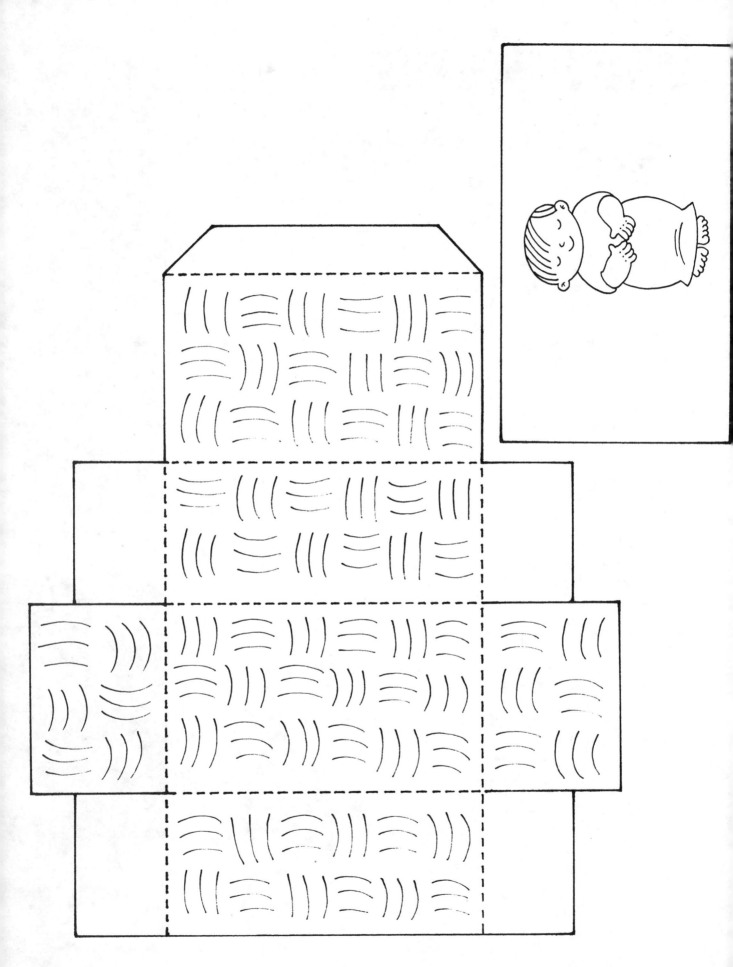

The Burning Bush

Game

Supplies: feet (see page 30), colored construction paper, pen, masking tape

On Holy Ground

Before the children arrive, make multiple copies of the feet (see page 30) so that you can create a lengthy trail around the room. Periodically interrupt the trail with a piece of colored construction paper.

On the construction paper write a question or have the children do something that relates to the Bible or Bible stories with which the children may be familiar. The children will have to answer the question or provide the information before they can move on. Use questions or activities such as these: What are the two parts of the Bible? (*Old Testament and New Testament*) Name two books of the Old Testament. Name two books of the New Testament. Name a Bible story from the Old Testament. Name one of Jesus' disciples.

Plan questions and activities around the skills you feel are appropriate to your class.

Direct the children to follow the path so that they can go on to "holy ground."

Ask: What do you think "holy ground" is? (*Invite the children to think about what this expression means.*) Who would be present on "holy ground." (*God*) How would you know God is there?

Say: Today we're talking about a person in the Bible who encounters God in a special place. But we know that we can find God everywhere.

© 1998 Abingdon Press.

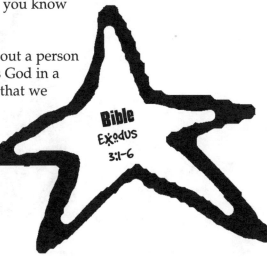

Bible
Exodus
3:1-6

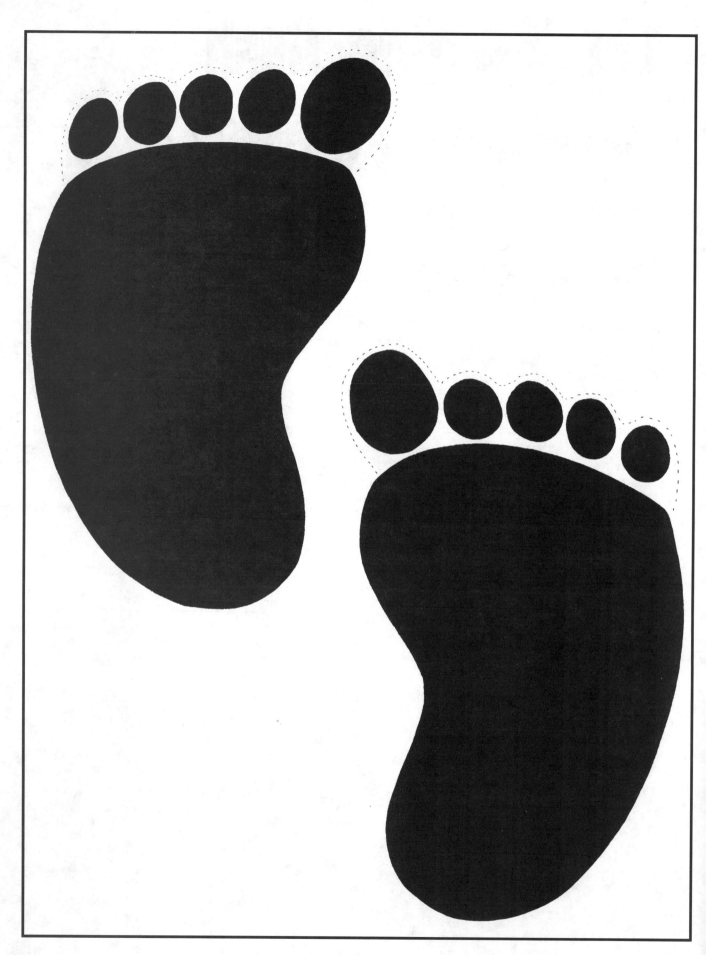

Let My People Go!

Game 1

Impossible Jump

Say: It seemed like an easy job. Go to Egypt. Talk to the king. Tell him to let the people go. But Moses knew better. He knew he needed God's help. Let's try a job that seems simple.

Ask: Can I see you jump? (*Invite the children to jump flat-footed. Then let them jump on one foot. If you have an older group, let them jump backwards.*)

Say: Let's try it again. But this time I want you to hold onto your toes as you jump. (*Have the children hold onto the toes of their shoes with both hands.*) Now jump! What's the matter? (*It's impossible to do.*) But it's so simple. I can't believe you can't do this. (*Let the children try again.*)

Then invite the children to get together in pairs and jump with the help of their partners.

Ask: Did it seem like a simple activity? What made it difficult? (*holding your toes*) Was it easier to do when you had help?

Bible
Exodus
5:1-2

Game 2

Supplies: chairs

Old Pharaoh Says

Say: We're going to pretend that we are the Hebrew people who are slaves in Egypt. One of you will be Pharaoh.

Choose one child to be Pharaoh. Pharaoh will stand in the center of the circle. Everyone will shout at Pharaoh, "Let my people go!" Each time Pharaoh will answer either "yes" or "no."

Say: If Pharaoh answers "no," then everyone remains seated, and we will ask again. If Pharaoh answers "yes," then each player must change places with another player.

Pharaoh tries to tag (or capture) one or more of the players while he or she is without a chair. Those players then join Pharaoh in the center of the circle, helping Pharaoh capture the Hebrew people.

Say: We have to be very careful because Pharaoh can be very sneaky.

As the game progresses, remove any empty chairs. When only one player remains, he or she becomes the next Pharaoh.

Say: Moses knew that he couldn't do the job alone. He needed God's help. With God's help, Moses freed the Hebrew people.

In the Wilderness

Game

Supplies: masking tape, blindfold, small sticky notes

On the Right Path

Use masking tape to lay out a trail around the center of the room. Make sure the trail is no wider than two feet. Provide turns in the trail that will require careful negotiation.

Select one of the children to be the marshal. If this creates an uneven number of children, let two children be marshals and station them on opposite sides of the game field. Divide the remaining children into teams of two.

Give each team a blindfold. Have the team members decide who is going to be the Trailwalker and who is going to be the Guide.

> **Say:** Today we will participate in a kind of trust walk. Instead of one person leading the other through the course, one person is going to guide the other person—not with words, but with a gentle touch on either the person's right or left shoulder. This will direct the Trailwalker in the appropriate direction. A touch on the right shoulder means turn to the right. A touch on the left shoulder means turn to the left. A touch in the center of the back means to go straight ahead. The marshal will call out, "Off the path!" if anyone steps outside the trail, and that team will then collect a ticket (small sticky note). Let's try to walk down the path without collecting any tickets. The team with the fewest tickets wins.

When the first player has made it down the right path, have the children switch places.

Bible
Exodus
15:22-16:35

The Ten Commandments

Game 1

Supplies: Ten Commandments (see pages 36 and 37), masking tape, beanbag

Commandment Capers

Make a copy of the Ten Commandments (see pages 36 and 37). Make sure each child has a commandment taped to him or her. Have the children stand in a circle. Put a masking tape X in the center of the circle.

Say: Look at your commandment very carefully. I am going to call out what the commandment says and then toss the beanbag high in the air. The person who is wearing that commandment must come and stand on that X before the beanbag hits the ground. If two people are wearing the same commandment, then they have to share the X.

Play until each child has had an opportunity to come forward.

© 1998 Abingdon Press.

Game 2

Supplies: six balloons, permanent felt-tip marker

Comin' At Ya!

Prior to class blow up six balloons. Using a permanent felt-tip marker, write one of these phrases on each balloon: tell a lie, disobey, be unkind, steal, use bad language, cheat.

Bible
Exodus
20:1-17

Bring the children in a circle.

Say: Every day we have temptations coming at us. (*Pitch a balloon to one of the children and have him or her keep the balloon moving.*) Some are easy to deal with. (*Pitch another balloon into the circle.*) Some are not so easy to deal with. (*Pitch another balloon into the circle.*) They just keep on coming day after day after day. (*Pitch the remainder of the balloons into the circle.*) Sometimes we choose to do what's right, but it isn't always easy to do. But God wants to help us know what's right. (*Keep the balloons going for a few minutes.*)

Stop the balloons. Have a child hold up a balloon, read the words, and tell when he or she might have been tempted to do this. Do not force any child to contribute if he or she feels uncomfortable.

Say: God gave us a set of rules that would help us know how to live. They are called the Ten Commandments. When God sent Jesus into the world, God was trying to help the people get back to following the law as God intended.

Make a copy of a simplified version of the Ten Commandments to go in your classroom. Talk about what these rules mean: You shall have no other gods before me. Worship only God. Do not use God's name in a wrongful way. Keep the sabbath day holy. Honor your father and mother. You shall not murder. Be faithful to your marriage vows. Do not steal. Do not lie. Do not want what belongs to your neighbor.

© 1997 Abingdon Press.

Game 3

I Spy

Say: Let's see what kind of watchers and guessers you are. Moses saw an unusual sight high up on a mountaintop. I am going to look around the room and identify an object. You have ten chances to find out what it is. You can ask ten questions, each of which must be able to be answered "yes" or "no." The one who guesses gets to be the next spy.

Select an object in the room. Then hold up ten fingers. As the children guess, fold down your fingers until there are no more fingers left. If the children cannot guess, tell them what the object is and select a child to be the next spy.

© 1998 Abingdon Press.

1 You shall have no other Gods before me.

2 You shall not make an idol and worship it.

3 You shall not make wrongful use of the name of the LORD your God.

8 You shall not steal.

7 You shall not commit adultery.

6 You shall not murder.

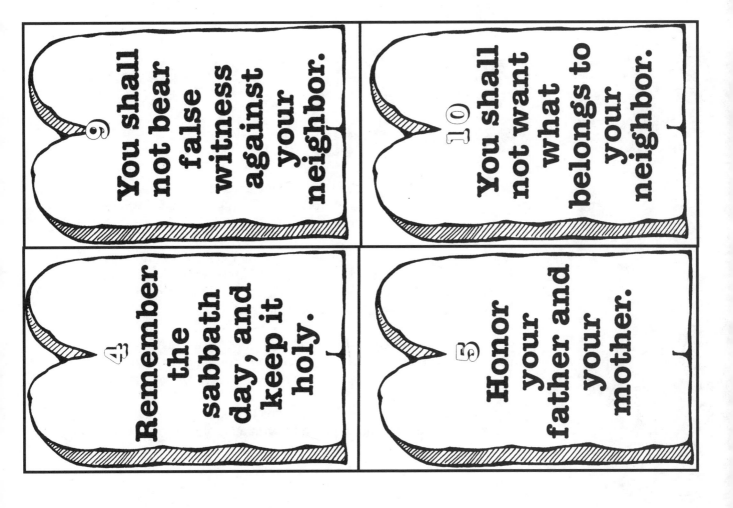

9 You shall not bear false witness against your neighbor.

10 You shall not want what belongs to your neighbor.

4 Remember the sabbath day, and keep it holy.

5 Honor your father and your mother.

Joshua and the Battle of Jericho

Game

Nose and Toes

Say: Joshua says touch your knee. Joshua says touch your ear. Joshua says hop in place. Joshua says touch the floor. Joshua says run in place. Stop. Joshua says stop.

Say: Those were pretty easy. Let's try again. Joshua says jump up and down. Joshua says stop. Joshua says jump up and touch the ceiling. (*Let the children try to jump higher and higher.*) What's the matter? (*It's impossible to touch the ceiling simply by jumping.*)

Say: Joshua says touch your nose to your toes. Joshua says touch your nose to your finger. Joshua says touch your nose to your elbow. What's the matter? (*It's impossible to touch your nose to your elbow.*)

Say: Some things seem impossible for us to do. The Bible tells a story about a man who did the impossible, with a lot of help from God.

Bible
Joshua
6:2-20

Ruth and Naomi

Game 1

Stuck Like Glue

Say: Today we're talking about a person by the name of Ruth. She is the daughter-in-law of a woman named Naomi. That means she was married to Naomi's son. Ruth shows Naomi just how much she loves her by "sticking with her" through thick and thin, even though she didn't have to. Ruth "stuck" because she really loved Naomi and cared about what happened to her.

Say: Let's play a game where we "stick" together. To start off you are stuck together by hands.

Divide the children into partners. Have the children stand in a circle next to their partners. The leader will stand in the center of the circle. Begin to repeat, "I love you, so we're stuck like glue." Encourage the children to join in.

After repeating the phrase several times, substitute the name of body parts for the phrase "like glue," keeping the same basic rhythm. As the players repeat the phrase, they assume the position with their partners that was suggested by the phrase. For example, if nose to shoulder was called, one partner will touch his or her nose to the other partner's shoulder.

The game will continue until everyone has assumed the position. Then the leader will call out another set of body parts (shoulder to ankle, knee to chin, chin to back, ear to nose, and so forth). When the leader calls, "Change!", everyone will have to scamper around and find a new partner. When each child has found his or her new partner, re-form the circle and begin again.

Begin with simple commands and then get more complicated. You may want to write down the commands before beginning, so you don't have to think about them as the game goes on.

Bible
Ruth
1–4

Game 2

May I Go With You?

Select one child to be Naomi. Have the class make a circle around Naomi.

Naomi will decide on a special criteria for selecting followers, such as: persons wearing red, persons with an "R" in their names, persons who have glasses, and so forth. Naomi will walk around the inside of the circle.

When Naomi stands in front of a child, that child will ask: "May I go with you?" If that child meets her criteria, Naomi will nod, and that child will stand behind Naomi.

When a child in the group decides he or she knows what the criteria is for going with Naomi, he or she raises a hand and makes a guess. If this guess is correct, that child becomes the next Naomi.

After three or four children are following behind Naomi, if no one has guessed, let the child pretending to be Naomi share her or his criteria and choose another Naomi. When everyone has had a chance to be Naomi or the children begin to lose interest, end the game.

Ask: What was the criteria Naomi used to let Ruth go with her? (*Ruth loved her mother-in-law and wanted to take care of her.*)

© 1999 Abingdon Press.

Samuel's Call

Game 1

Supplies: masking tape or yarn, whistle

Listen Up!

Bring the children together in an open area. Create a safety zone in an area of the room. Mark it either with masking tape or yarn.

Say: When we are listening for God's call, we had better be good listeners.

Play a game that requires the children to listen and to follow directions. Choose one child to be the caller. Tell the rest of the children that they will be part of the group.

Say: Over there is an area called the safety zone. In the safety zone, you can't be tagged. In this game we are going to form groups of different sizes. You will have to listen very carefully and pay attention. When I say, "Sprawl," everyone begins to hop around until you hear the whistle blow.

Have the caller call out a number between two and five. The children must run to form groups of that number before they are tagged by the caller.

Say: If you're left without a group, run to the safety zone.

The first person tagged becomes the next caller.

Bible
1 Samuel
3:1-10

Game 2

How Do You Know?

Ask: How did God talk to Samuel? (*Samuel heard God's voice.*) How does God talk to us? (*Invite the children to share how they think God can talk to us today.*) How do we know what God wants us to do?

Say: We can listen for God's voice. Sometimes we can hear God as we read the Bible. Sometimes we can hear God as we listen to Sunday school teachers or pastors. Sometimes we hear God through loving adults who care for us.

Tell the children that you are going to name some things that boys and girls can do.

Say: If you think that these are things that God might call us to do, hold your hand like a telephone (*thumb and pinky finger extended, middle three fingers folded down*) and say, "Ringy dingy." If you think it is something that God definitely would not call us to do, then make the rejection buzzer sound. If an activity is neither one, shrug your shoulders.

Volunteer to help with Special Olympics on Saturday. (*ringy dingy*)
Skip church and go swimming instead. (*buzzer*)
Go to the movies on Sunday afternoon. (*shrug*)
Collect blankets for the homeless. (*ringy dingy*)
Spread a rumor about a classmate. (*buzzer*)
Participate in a charity walk-a-thon. (*ringy dingy*)
Play with friends in the park. (*shrug*)
Spend your church money on ice cream. (*buzzer*)
Do extra chores for your grandmother, who's sick. (*ringy dingy*)
Laugh at the weird clothes of a new kid in school. (*buzzer*)

Samuel Finds David

Game

Who's the One?

Say: God knew who the new king would be. God knew David from the inside out. Let's see if we know one another that well.

Select one child to be IT. Have IT leave the room or face the wall while you select one child to be the heart. Invite IT to turn back around.

Say: It is up to you to find out who's the one. You will ask the whole group the question, "Who's the one?" The person who is the heart must go "thump, thump," just like a heart. Let's practice a couple of times.

Have IT ask the question and have the whole class make the thumping sound of the heart. Then have the children cup their hands over their mouths.

When the game starts, only the child who has been selected makes the sound.

Every time IT asks, "Who's the one?" the person that the teacher selected has to answer, "thump, thump." IT can ask this three times. If IT doesn't guess who it is, IT has to do it again. If IT discovers who's the one, then the two will trade places.

Bible
I Samuel
16:1-13

43

David and Goliath

Game

Supplies: masking tape, chair, ping-pong ball, whistle

Balancing Act

Use masking tape to designate a starting point. Have the children form a line behind the starting point. Place a chair about ten feet from the starting point. The children will face the chair.

Give the first child a ping-pong ball.

Say: I will blow the whistle to start. You will place the ping-pong ball on the back of your hand and walk around the chair and back to the line. Then pass the ball to the next person in line. If the ball falls off, pick it up and put it back on. But that is the only time you may touch the ball with your hands. The object of the game is for everyone to go around the chair before I blow the whistle again.

Note for the Teacher: If you have a large class (more than ten children), use more than one ball. Don't try to set up competition between teams. The idea is for everyone to participate and to have fun.

Make sure all the children are standing in line. Place the ball on the hand of the first child. Blow the whistle and begin the game. Allow an adequate amount of time for the children to finish. After the game pick up the ball(s) and put them away.

Have the children sit down.

Ask: Was the game fun to play? Was it easy or hard? (*hard*) What made it hard? (*having to use the backs of hands*) What might have made it easier? (*using hands palms up instead*) Would that have been as much fun?

Bible
I Samuel
17:1–50

David and Jonathan

Game 1

Supplies: large piece of paper, marker, beach ball

Deflection Protection

Ask: What are some of the things that friends do for one another?

Make a list of those things on a large piece of paper. Make sure to include, "Friends look out for one another."

Say: Here we've listed that friends look out for one another. Let's play a game where this is true. The object of the game is for the people in the circle to hit the person in the middle with the beach ball. It is the friend's job to make sure this doesn't happen. One friend is the Protector; the other friend is the Dodger. Get together and decide who will be whom in your team.

The group will form a circle. The first pair of friends will stand in the center. Hand one of the children in the circle the beach ball. That person will try to bop the Dodger while the Protector tries to protect the Dodger.

Make sure each pair of friends has a chance to be in the center.

Bible
1 Samuel
18:1-4

45

Game 2

Supplies: yarn, unbreakable items from the classroom, blindfold

Fieldguide Frenzy

Say: Friends help one another. Let's play a game where one friend will help another get through a dangerous field of obstacles. One of the friends will be blindfolded. The other friend will use verbal clues to guide the second friend safely through the field.

Make a circle with a twenty-foot piece of yarn. Inside the yarn arrange several items from your classroom. Make sure the items are unbreakable.

Let the pairs decide who is going to be the crawler and who is going to be the guide. When the crawler gets from one side of the circle to the other, the crawler becomes the guide and the guide the crawler. If a crawler bumps into an object, he or she must leave the field and get in line to try again. Make sure the children have an opportunity to be both. If you have a large class, create more than one circle so several teams can play at one time.

© 1998 Abingdon Press.

Game 3

Supplies: balloons, masking tape or yarn

Balloon Sandwich

Say: David and Jonathan were great friends. Jonathan was ready to risk his position as prince to protect his friend David. He was even willing to risk his life. David remembered even when he was king how Jonathan had helped him. Now let's play a game where friends help one another.

Blow up a balloon for each pair of friends. Mark a beginning line and an ending line with either masking tape or yarn. Have the children hold the balloon between them back to back.

The friends must move from a starting point to an ending point while holding the balloon between their backs. If the balloon falls down, they start again.

Say: Today we have learned that friends love one another. When friends love one another, that means they care, they share, they help, they look out for, and they show appreciation for one another.

46

© 1998 Abingdon Press.

House of the Lord

Game

Supplies: Temple furnishings (see page 48), scissors, chairs

Inside/Outside

Make a copy of the furnishings for the Temple (see page 48). Cut apart the cards and give one to each child. Have the children bring their chairs into a circle. Go around the circle and have each child hold up her or his card and read the name that is printed beneath.

Have each child hold up his or her picture as you describe each of the items that would have been found in Solomon's Temple.

Say: Outside the Temple was a bronze basin, called a "sea," supported by statues of twelve oxen. The priests purified themselves in this basin. Also outside was an altar for burnt offerings. To the side of the Temple were wheeled dollies with basins of water for washing sacrificial animals. There were five on each side. There were two pillars on the front of the building. They were named Jachin and Boaz, but no one now knows why. At the front of the Temple were two large olive wood doors. Carved into these doors were winged creatures, palm trees, and open flowers.

Continue: One of the first things in the Temple was a golden table where twelve new loaves of bread were laid each week. Nearby was a golden altar where priests burned incense. On each side of the room were five lamp stands that gave off a soft glow against the golden walls. You would find the Ark of the Covenant, a gold chest that contained the clay tablets of the Ten Commandments, at the back of the Temple in the Holy of Holies. No one was allowed there except the priest. Guarding the Ark of the Covenant were two winged creatures called cherubim.

Let the children play a game.

Say: One of you will be IT and will be the builder of the Temple. IT will call out one of the items from the Temple. If you are holding that item, you will come to the center of the circle. When IT says "It's finished!", then all of you will try to get back to your seats. At the same time IT will be trying to get your chair. The one left without a chair will become the next IT.

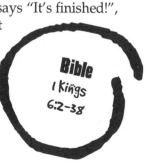

Bible
1 Kings
6:2-38

Play until all the children have had a chance to be IT or as long as the children show interest.

Ten Commandments

Bronze Sea

Oil Lamp

Bread Table

Bronze Pillar (Boaz)

Incense Altar

Ark of the Covenant

Burnt Offering Altar

Bronze Pillar (Jachin)

Wheeled Basin

Cherubim

Olive Wood Doors

Thank You, God

Game

Supplies: newspapers, oversized sweatshirts, cassette or CD, cassette or CD player

Stuffed With Praise

Say: There are so many things we can say thank you to God for giving us. Let's see just how big our praises can be.

Divide the children into groups of three or four children. Give each group a stack of newspapers.

Have the groups each select one person from that group to be "stuffed with praise." The rest of the children will be the stuffers. The one being stuffed will put on the oversized sweatshirt for her or his team and stand in the middle of the group.

Say: While the music plays, we are going to take turns praising God for all the wonderful things of creation. Each time you mention something, you wad up a sheet of newspaper and stuff the newspaper ball inside the sweatshirt worn by the person in the middle. Let's see just how "stuffed with praise" that person will become. Remember, you can't stuff a wad of newspaper without praising God for some part of God's creation. Everyone has to say something different each time around.

Play music on a cassette or CD as the children do the stuffing. When the song ends, have the "stuffed shirts" parade around the room. Then let the children remove the sweatshirts and put the wadded-up newspaper in the trash.

Ask: What did you discover as you played this game? (*That we have much for which to praise God.*)

© 1999 Abingdon Press.

Bible
Psalm
9:1

49

Jeremiah

Game 1

Supplies: beach ball

Good News Message

Have the children stand in a line one behind the other.

Say: It is our job to get the good news message (*Hold up a beach ball.*) to everyone. The first person in line will pass the beach ball over her or his head. The second person will pass the beach ball between his or her legs. The third person will pass the beach ball over her or his head and so on, until the beach ball comes to the last person in line. That person will take the beach ball and run to the front, beginning the game again.

When everyone has a chance to begin the relay, have the children sit down.

Ask: Was it fun to pass the good news from one person to another? The prophet Jeremiah wanted to pass the good news to all the people, but he kept having problems. Not everyone wanted to hear what he had to say.

Game 2

Supplies: colored construction paper, blindfold, masking tape

Through the Zone

Bring the children together in an open space. Divide them into two lines. One line will be the Jeremiahs; the other line will be the people of Israel. Each Jeremiah will give directions to one of the people of Israel, to help God's people get through the Danger Zone (open space in the center of the room) without stepping on a colored piece of construction paper. The person representing the people of Israel will be blindfolded.

Arrange the construction paper so that the squares form a random pattern in the open space. Secure to the floor with masking tape. The open space is the Danger Zone. The colored squares of construc-

Bible
Jeremiah
1:4–10

tion paper are the enemy.

If the child who is acting as the people of Israel steps on a colored square, he or she has been captured by the Babylonians, and the next Jeremiah takes over. The next person from the people of Israel will put on the blindfold and listen for directions.

> **Say:** God called Jeremiah to be a prophet when he was a boy. God wanted Jeremiah to tell the people that they were living in the Danger Zone. If they didn't listen and change their direction, they were going to be in trouble. The enemy nations surrounded them. If they didn't return to the Lord, they would become captives. No matter what happened, Jeremiah always seemed to run afoul of the law. The king thought Jeremiah was a troublemaker and wanted him to be quiet. I want those of you who are Jeremiah to stand on opposite sides of the room. You will shout out directions to your partner. Your partner can only move one step at a time. It is up to Jeremiah to get the people of Israel through the Danger Zone to the other side.

Play until every child has a chance to be Jeremiah or the people of Israel. Once everyone has had a chance to be one or the other, have the children swap places if you have a small class. The person who is Jeremiah will shout out directions, such as "Take one baby step forward," "Take one giant step forward," or "Step sideways to the right." The idea is for the person who is blindfolded to listen to Jeremiah so that he or she can get through the Danger Zone without being captured.

> **Ask:** Was it difficult to get through the maze? (*You had to listen carefully to the directions.*) What happened if you didn't listen? (*You were captured.*)

Game 3

Supplies: cassette or CD, cassette or CD player

Jeremiah Jump

Bring the children together in the open space.

> **Say:** God called Jeremiah and gave him a special job. Jeremiah was to tell the people to return to God. Jeremiah took his job seriously, even though it meant that he was arrested, thrown in a well, and otherwise treated badly. Jeremiah knew he had to keep on telling others what God wanted them to hear. I am going to play music. I want you to do the Jeremiah Bullfrog Jump. (*Squat down and leap up.*) When the music stops, you must stop. I will name a color. If you are wearing that color, tell the group something you know about God. When each person wearing the specified color has contributed, I will start the music again and everyone will begin to jump.

Start and stop the music often enough that you can name several colors. Play until each child has had a chance to contribute. If the children have a difficult time getting started, you may want to give them some suggestions, such as: "God made the world," "God loves me," or "God watches over us."

Potters

Game

Sculptor and Clay

Bring the children together in an open area. Divide them into pairs. Have the pairs decide which one will be the artist and which will become the clay.

Say: Sculptor, in front of you is a very posable lump of clay. It is your job to create your finest sculpture from this clay. Clay, you are the finest clay available. You will hold whatever shape your sculptor can imagine.

Or have the sculptor form the clay without touching it. The sculptor may use only words. Words the sculptor might use are: "Bend at the wrist," "Stretch your arm toward the ceiling," or "Open your mouth."

When the masterpiece is completed, the sculptor will show his or her work to the rest of the class or group. Then the partners will reverse roles and the artistic process will begin again.

Bible
Jeremiah
18:1-6

Daniel and the Lions

Game 1

Think Difficult

Ask: What is the most difficult thing you can think of to do?

Have the children take turns and act it out. Let the other class members try to guess.

Give the children a minute or two to come up with something—climbing a mountain, driving a car, doing math problems, cleaning windows, practicing the piano.

Say: The Bible tells us about a man named Daniel, who has to do something very, very hard. He has to choose whether or not to be faithful to God. That doesn't seem very difficult, but it is.

Bible
Daniel
6:10-26

Game 2

Supplies: masking tape

Work Together

Use masking tape to make a circle or square on the floor. Then make a circle or square of similar size about ten feet away. Place items from the classroom in one of the areas. Have the children stand in a line.

Say: The object of this game is to move each item from one area to the other area—one item at a time. Each person has one minute. When the minute is over, I will blow the whistle, and the next person takes over.

Designate one child as the beginning player. Then as if you just happened to remember, **say:** Get ready, get set, oh, wait a minute. I forgot to tell you. There's a catch. You can't use your hands. Now go!

Allow each child thirty seconds to one minute; then the next child gets to try. Play until each child has had an opportunity to try to move the items. Have the children sit down in a circle.

Ask: At first, did this game seem to be easy? What made it hard? How did you feel when you couldn't use your hands to move the items from place to place?

Say: Today we're talking about a man who is faced with doing something very difficult. He is called upon to be faithful, but he's having a hard time.

NEW TESTAMENT

Wise Men's Visit

Game 1

Supplies: paper, marker, three items from your classroom

Give Me a Sign

Before class begins, select one child to be in on the trick to this game. If you have a very young group of children, you may want to ask another adult to participate instead.

Write one of these letters on one of three plain sheets of paper: C, A, R. Place the sheets of paper on the floor. Have the children form a circle with the three pieces of paper in the center. Place an item from the classroom on C, a second item on A, and a third item on R.

   Say: A secret sign told some people who study the stars that a new king had been born. I wonder how they knew. Let's play a game where there is a secret sign. Only (*name of child*) and I know what it is. See if you can discover what it is.

Secret sign: The words the leader uses to call the child back to the group will identify which item has been chosen. "Come back" means the group has chosen the item on C. "All right" means the group has chosen the item on A. "Ready!" means the group has chosen the item on R.

   Say: Pay close attention.

Have the selected child leave the circle or turn away. Have one of the children select one of the items. Then recall the child to the group using the secret code. (*Come in, All right, Ready*)

   Ask: Which item do you think the group has chosen?

Do this several times so that the children are mystified and trying to discover the secret code. If no one figures it out, let the child explain it to the group.

   Say: IT was listening for a special sign to help him/her know which item the group had chosen. Some scholars were watching for a secret sign as well. When they saw the new star, they knew that a new king had been born. This king was not just for one group of people or country; this king had come for all people.

Bible
Matthew
2:1-11

Game 2
Secret Signs

Bring the children together. Have them be seated in their chairs and form a circle. (If you have limited space, this can be done around a table where the chairs have been pushed back.)

Say: We are going to play a game of secret signs. When I make the secret signs, everyone will do what the sign tells you to do. Everyone will move over one chair to the right when I pull my earlobe. (*Pull your earlobe and let everyone move one chair to the right.*) Everyone will move over one chair to the left when I touch my nose. (*Touch your nose and let everyone shift one chair to the left.*) Everyone will stand up when I scratch my chin. (*Scratch your chin and let everyone stand up.*) Is everyone ready? (*You may want to practice one more time, and mix the signs up to get the children's attention.*)

Talk with the children about their experiences of the past week. Talk about their pets and their families. During the conversation, very subtly make the secret signs. Keep everyone moving. Quit after a few minutes.

Say: Today we're hearing about some people who saw a secret sign. The sign told them what had happened and what they should do. The sign was the symbol that told them a new king had been born, and they went to find the king

© 1999 Abingdon Press.

Game 3

Supplies: balloon

Royal Ruckus

Have the children stand in a circle and hold hands.

Say: The star was a sign that the new king had been born. The magi saw the star and set out in search of the new king. God's people had been waiting for a long time for the Savior, the Messiah. God didn't send Jesus just to the Hebrews—God sent Jesus to everyone. Let's see if all of us, together, can keep that star shining.

Toss a balloon into the air. Players will attempt to keep the balloon from hitting the ground by using any parts of their bodies that may be necessary. The round will end when the balloon touches the ground or when two players disconnect their hands.

© 1999 Abingdon Press.

57

The Beatitudes

Game 1

Are You Happy, Fox?

Have the children come to an open area of the room. Create a safety zone at one end of the room and the Fox's Den at the other end of the room. Have all the children but one stand in the safety zone. Select one child to be Fox. Have Fox stand in the den facing away from the safety zone. The object of the game is for the children to see how close they can get to Fox before he turns around and catches them.

The players will take steps out of the safety zone toward the fox. Each time the group will ask, "Are you happy, Fox?" Fox will answer, "No, I'm sad," or "No, I'm tired," or "No, I'm angry." If Fox answers, "Yes, I'm happy," then Fox turns around and tries to catch the children before they get back to the safety zone.

Say: Everyone wants to be happy. But there are just times when we don't feel happy. Jesus knew this. But he also knew that God wants us to be happy and that when we are with God, we will always be happy.

Ask: Can you walk happy? What does a happy walk look like? What does a sad walk look like? How do you walk when you're angry? How do you walk when you're tired? How do you walk when you're scared? (*Pause after each question and give the children an opportunity to imitate the feelings in their walks.*)

Bible
Matthew
5:3-12

Game 2

All for One!

Have the children form groups of four. Count off and let all the "ones" go to one corner of the room; all the "twos" will go to the opposite corner; and the "threes" and "fours" will go to the remaining corners.

Try to create at least two groups, if you have a small class. If this is not possible, simply have one group.

Say: Today we're hearing about a very joyful event. At the time everyone agreed that it was the most joyful thing that had ever happened and that would ever happen. Even today everyone agrees. Everybody likes to be joyful and happy. But not everyone agrees upon just what makes him or her happy. Everyone in your group in this game must agree on one thing that makes all of you happy. For example, I'll ask: "What makes you happy at school?" Your group must find an answer you all agree on. If even one person doesn't agree, you must find another answer. It's not as easy as it sounds. As soon as your team agrees, shout it out to let us know you've come to an agreement.

Use the following situations for the children to try to agree upon:

What makes you happy in the summer?
What makes you happy at church?
What makes you happy on your birthday?
What makes you happy in the morning?
What makes you happy in the evening?

Say: It's not always easy to agree on everything.

Bible—Times Homes

Game

Supplies: Bible-times tools (see page 61), scissors

Tool Time

Make a copy of the Bible-times tools (see page 61) for each table of children. Cut the tools apart and spread them out on the table where they can be easily seen by everyone.

Say: In Bible times persons built buildings just as they do today. But they look a little different.

Ask: How do you think the buildings are different? (*Bible-times buildings aren't as tall; people in Bible times did not have steel or concrete to use in building them; there was no electricity in Bible times for power tools.*) But still they had tools they used to make the buildings the best that they could. I am going to describe how a particular tool is used. In front of you are eight tools that would have been used in Bible times. When you think you know the answer as a group, select one person to pick up that picture and run with it to the front.

Even though the trees in Palestine did not grow very tall and straight, still a carpenter had to cut them into boards for doors and tables and benches. He probably used this. (*saw*)

In order to know how tall and how wide to make a door, the carpenter in Bible times used this to measure. (*rule stick*)

If a wall was not made straight, it might fall down. A carpenter used this weight and string to make sure the wall was straight. (*plummet and line*)

A carpenter would use this tool to help him draw a true circle. (*compass*)

Carpenters often need to make holes in pieces of wood for pegs. A carpenter might use this tool, drawing one part back and forth over the other, causing it to make a hole. (*bow drill*)

Stone blocks did not come cut to size. Sometimes a carpenter used this tool to take off small chunks of stone or wood so that the blocks would fit more snugly. (*chisel*)

The carpenter used this tool to pound iron nails into the wood. (*mallet*)

A carpenter would not want his customers to get splinters in their behinds, so he would use this to smooth down the rough edges of

Bible
Matthew
7:24-27

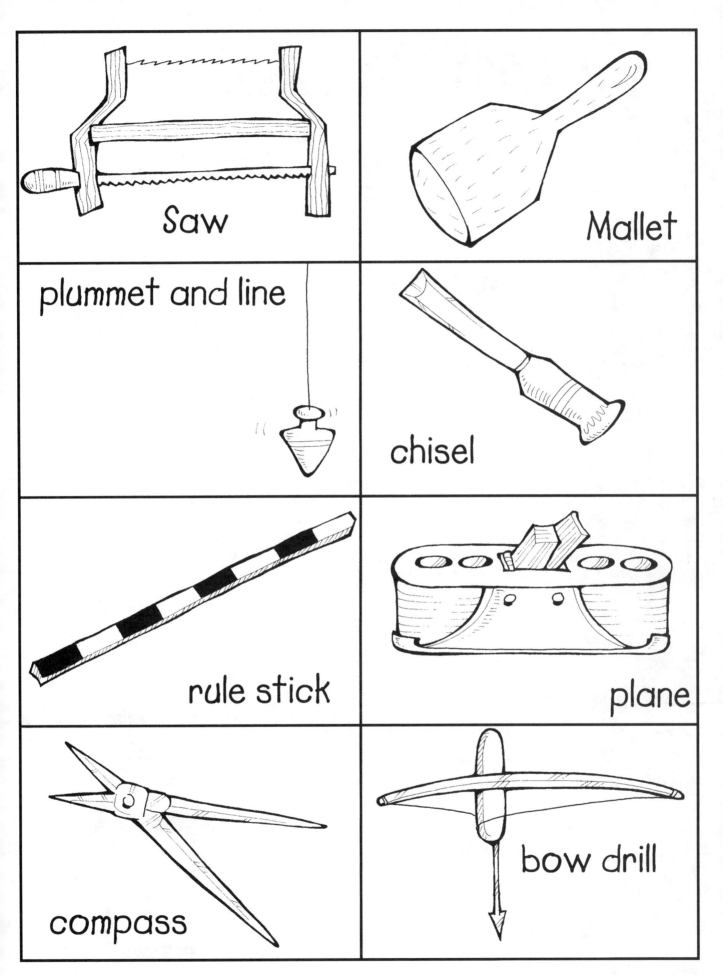

Saw

Mallet

plummet and line

chisel

rule stick

plane

compass

bow drill

Levi/Matthew

Game 1

Supplies: cardboard tubes

Stop, Thief!

Gather the children in an open space. Select one child to be the tax collector. The rest of the children will be the villagers. Have the children stand shoulder to shoulder with their hands behind their backs. Hold up a cardboard tube.

Say: Even though this doesn't look like it, this is a valuable item. It is all you have in the world. You would like to keep it, but the tax collector wants to get it.

Walk behind the circle, placing a cardboard tube in each child's hands. Tell him or her not to grip the tube, but to just let it rest there.

Say: The tax collector is going to wander through the village and decide which person's wealth he or she is going to steal. When the tax collector steals your wealth, then you will shout out: "Stop, thief!" and chase the tax collector before he or she runs around the circle and comes back to your spot. If you catch the tax collector, you get your wealth back. If not, then you become the next tax collector.

Make sure there are no obstacles that will cause injury as the children run. When everyone has had a chance to be either a victim or a tax collector, have the children sit down where they are.

Say: Today we're hearing about a dishonest tax collector. Not only does he take the money that is due, he takes more than his share. How do you think the people feel about him? How would you feel about him? But Jesus knew that down inside Levi was a good person and if given a second chance, would live a better life. Jesus knew that God loved and forgave Levi.

Bible
Matthew
9:9–13

Game 2

Supplies: magazines, scissors, large brown mailing envelope

A Part Is Not a Whole

Prior to class, remove pictures from magazines. Choose pictures that are large and colorful and, if possible, of a single item, such as a pet or a person or an item such as a car. Take a large brown mailing envelope. Somewhere on the top of the envelope cut a small hole, a circle or square about one inch across. Slip the magazine pictures inside.

Hold up the envelope where the children can see it. Pass it around the circle.

Ask: Can you tell what the picture is just by looking at one small part of it? Why not? (*A small part is not the whole thing.*)

Pass each picture all around the circle and let the children try to guess what the picture is. After everyone has had a chance to guess, remove the picture from the envelope and hold it up for the children to see. Do this with all the pictures.

Say: Just as you can't tell what the total picture looks like from just a small part of it, you can't tell what a person is like by just knowing a little bit about him or her. The Bible tells us a story about people in a village who have formed an opinion about a person because he is a tax collector. But this is only a small part of who he is. Jesus knew all about him and about the person he could become.

Say: In Bible times, the Romans ruled the country where Jesus lived. The Roman king wanted to build great monuments, wonderful roads, a strong army, and aqueducts to bring water from the mountains. All of this building required money. So the king raised the money by taxing all the countries that the Roman army had defeated and now ruled. The Jewish people didn't like the Romans anyway. They didn't want them in their country at all. But when they started taxing the people, that was too much. And a tax collector, one of their fellow Jews, who worked for the Romans was lower than dirt. That's why it surprised the people when Jesus picked such a man to be one of his followers.

Jesus Calls Fishermen

Game 1

Supplies: masking tape

Join the Disciple—Ship

Use masking tape to make a ship shape on the floor big enough for everyone to stand inside.

Say: I've made an outline of a ship, a Disciple-Ship. We are living as disciples of Jesus whenever we try to live as Jesus taught, and whenever we follow Jesus' example. We are aboard the Disciple-Ship. I want you to think of a way you can be a disciple of Jesus in the coming week. As you think of something, shout it out, and I will invite you to "Get on board." We will cheer when everyone is on the Disciple-Ship.

Let the children make suggestions. Give them hints if they need them: sharing toys, caring for persons who are sick, helping older persons, doing an act of kindness, saying something nice to another person, and so forth.

© 1999 Abingdon Press.

Game 2

Supplies: masking tape

Swim, Fish, Swim!

Say: The first persons Jesus chose to be his helpers were four fishermen who had fishing businesses on the Sea of Galilee. Fish was a major food for people in Bible times. The job of a fisherman was important because of this. There

Bible
Mark
1:16–20

were no refrigerators, so fresh fish had to be caught every day. These fishermen used nets to catch their fish rather than using fishing poles. Sometimes they threw the nets out from the shore. Other times they threw the nets out from their boats on the lake.

Create safe harbors on opposite sides of the room using masking tape. Have the children line up horizontally at one side of the playing area behind the masking tape line. Choose one player to be the fisherman. The fisherman will stand in the center of the playing area and call out: "I'm a fisherman, as you can see. So come, little fish, come swimming to me." All the players will then run to the opposite side of the area. Those tagged by the fisherman join hands and then form a net to catch the other fish.

Only the two ends may tag, and the net must not be broken. Fish may swim through the net in the center and to the other side if not tagged. The last one caught is the fisherman for the next game.

Game 3

Supplies: large scarf

Catching People

Bring the children together in an open area of the room.

> **Ask:** How do you think Simon Peter, Andrew, James, and John are going to catch people? Do you think they'll use a net? Will they use a fishing pole and hook with worms? What do you think Jesus meant by catching people? What will the four men do to catch people?

Have the children stand and each child take hold of an edge of a large scarf. Have them hold the scarf high so there is space for children to stand beneath. Select one child to be the fisherman. Have the fisherman call out the names of children one at a time. The children will stand under the scarf.

Then the fisherman begins to count backward from ten. On zero, the fisherman calls out, "Haul it in!" The children holding onto the scarf lower it, trapping the "fish" inside. The object is for the fish to escape the "net" before it is lowered. Caution the children about getting too physical.

> **Say:** Simon Peter, Andrew, James, and John didn't use a net to catch people as we just did. They would travel with Jesus and let him be their teacher. Then they would tell others all that Jesus had told them. Through them, the good news about Jesus would spread to all the people.

Jesus Calms the Storm

Game 1

Supplies: cardboard and wax paper, or a large metal pizza pan; large scarf or short rope; tape

Lifeboat

Divide the classroom into three sections—the sinking boat, the stormy sea, and the lifeboat. The stormy sea section should not be wider than three feet. If you have a hardwood or tile floor, use a piece of cardboard approximately two feet square. (You may tape wax paper to the bottom to make it slide more easily.) If you are on a carpeted surface, use the cardboard or a large metal pizza pan. Choose one person to be captain of the lifeboat.

Say: Help! Help! The storm has sunk the boat. We need help—quick! Captain (*name of child*) has come to our rescue. But the captain can only rescue one person at a time. So get in line and be patient. But the captain only has (*number of minutes*) to get everyone off the boat. (*Gauge the amount of time this will take for the number of children you have.*)

The child you selected as IT will scoot the cardboard square or large metal pizza pan across the floor to where the children are waiting. She or he may come to the edge of the stormy sea, but must not step into it. The boys and girls in the sinking ship may come to the edge of the ship, but must not climb into the sea without the life boat. One child at a time will sit on the cardboard square or pizza pan. Then the captain will extend a large scarf or short rope for that person to hold onto. The captain will pull the person being rescued across the stormy sea. As each child is rescued, let that person cheer on the rescue of all the remaining children. If you have a large class, provide two life boats and two captains. Set a kitchen timer to count down the minutes.

Ask: Even though it was just pretend, how did it feel to be rescued? Did you feel relieved? Did you get nervous as the time began to run out? God sent Jesus into the world to save us. That is why we call Jesus our Lord and Savior. Jesus' disciples went to all the people they could to tell them about Jesus. The disciples wanted all the people to

Bible
Mark
4:35–39

be saved. Sometimes the disciples found themselves in strange places telling the story of Jesus.

Game 2

Supplies: whistle (optional: cassette or CD, cassette or CD player)

Freeze

Gather the children into a circle.

Say: When I blow the whistle, I want you to begin to dance around the room. Skip, hop, do whatever you feel like doing. But when you hear the whistle again, you have to stop where you are. Don't move a muscle. You can't begin moving again until I blow the whistle again. If you move after I have frozen you, you have to come and sit beside me. So watch carefully. Let's practice.

Start the game. After a few moments blow the whistle. Then start again. (Option: Use music as background as the children dance.) When you have a sizable collection of children who are out, stop the game.

Bring the children together on the floor or around a table.

Say: Being still after moving around is pretty hard. Today we're talking about something becoming still. When the disciples see this wonderful thing, they learn a very important lesson.

Game 3

Supplies: blindfold

Trust Me

Say: I am going to lead each of you around the room, one at a time. You will have to trust me because you will have on a blindfold.

Select one child to be first. One at a time, lead the children around the room. Have each child sit down. If a child has a problem with a blindfold, simply have him or her close his or her eyes. If you have a large class, pair the children and let them take turns leading each other around.

Ask: How did it feel to not know where you were going (*scary*) Did you trust me? (*your partner*) Did you think I would do anything that would hurt you? Why were you still afraid? (*It is hard to be trusting.*) Jesus' friends learned that they could depend upon God.

Bartimaeus

Game 1

Supplies: box or picnic basket

Pack a Picnic

Gather the children around a box that will serve as your imaginary picnic basket. (If you have a real picnic basket, this will add to the fun of the activity.) Ask the children if they have ever been on a picnic and where their favorite picnic spot is located. This is a good time to make important connections and to learn about each child's family situation.

This activity will help the children in attentive listening. The Bible character today had to do some attentive listening. When he recognized just who it was that was coming down the road, he decided to reach out to him.

> **Say:** We are going on a pretend picnic. As we pack our picnic basket, we will discover what kind of listeners you are. The object of the game is to recall what each person is putting in the picnic basket. As the basket is passed, the person who receives it will repeat what is already in the basket and then put in his or her own item before passing it to the next child on the right.

> **Say:** Today I'm packing my picnic basket, and I'll need some help. I'll put in some chocolate cake. What will you put in? (*Say the name of the child to your right and pass the basket to him or her.*) Each player repeats the articles already packed and adds his or her article.

> **Say:** Today we're talking about someone who listens very carefully, and he hears a person he has been wanting to meet. He has heard that this person can help him. Who do you think this person is? (*Jesus*)

> **Say:** Jesus does a special favor for this person. Through this favor Jesus teaches us something special. We also learn another special name for Jesus.

Bible
Mark
10:46-52

Game 2

Supplies: items for game (see page 72)

Rescue Me

Make a copy of the items for the game (see page 72). If you have more than eight children, make additional copies and let this be a game of competition as well. Arrange the chairs in a circle. Stand in the center of the circle.

Say: We are going to play "Rescue Me!" Each of you has an item that I might need. I will read a short statement. Listen carefully and decide just what it is that I need. When you think that you have the necessary item, rush it up here to me.

Help! It's raining, and I have to walk home from school. Help! (*umbrella*)
Help! My kitten is caught in the tree! Help! (*ladder*)
Help! My canoe is about to go over a waterfall! Help! (*oar*)
Help! This ship is sinking! Help! (*life preserver*)
Help! The plane is crashing! Help! (*parachute*)
Help! I'm in the desert, and I want to get home! Help! (*camel*)
Help! I want to get to the top of the cliff! Help! (*rope*)
Help! I need to get across the river! Help! (*bridge*)

Say: In each of the settings you gave me the help I needed. Can you think of times when we need Jesus' help? (*We need Jesus' help when we don't know what to do.*) Jesus promised that he would be our helper. He would show us what to do.

The Lord's Supper

Game 1

Supplies: index cards with the numbers one to five on them

Memory Scramble

Bring the children in a circle, with five children in the center. Let another child place the children in a particular order. Have everyone turn away; let the five children scramble themselves. Let someone put them back in order.

Then hand out index cards to the children in order—1-5. Have the children turn their backs; let the group of children scramble themselves. Placing them in order now is just a matter of putting the numbers in order.

Say: The numbers helped us get people in the right order. We often use objects and activities to remember. At church we use special things to help us remember.

Game 2

Supplies: bread and cup badge (see page 72), yarn, scissors, paper punch, whistle

Bread and Cup Tag

Photocopy and cut out a bread/cup badge (see page 72) for each child. Fold the badge so the bread and cup are back to back and tape shut. Cut a piece of yarn 20 inches long for each child. Punch a hole in the top of each badge. Attach the yarn to the badge. Give each child a badge. Have the children hang their badges around their necks.

Say: The bread and cup are two ways we remember Jesus. We use them at Holy Communion. We are going to play a game using our bread and cup badges. (*Have the children stand in a line. Count off A, B, A, B, A, and so forth.*) A's are bread. B's are cups. (*Have the children turn their badges appropriately.*) When I blow the whistle, breads try to tag cups. When a cup is tagged, he or she turns over the badge and becomes a bread. When I blow the whistle, cups try to tag the breads.

Bible
Mark
14:22-26

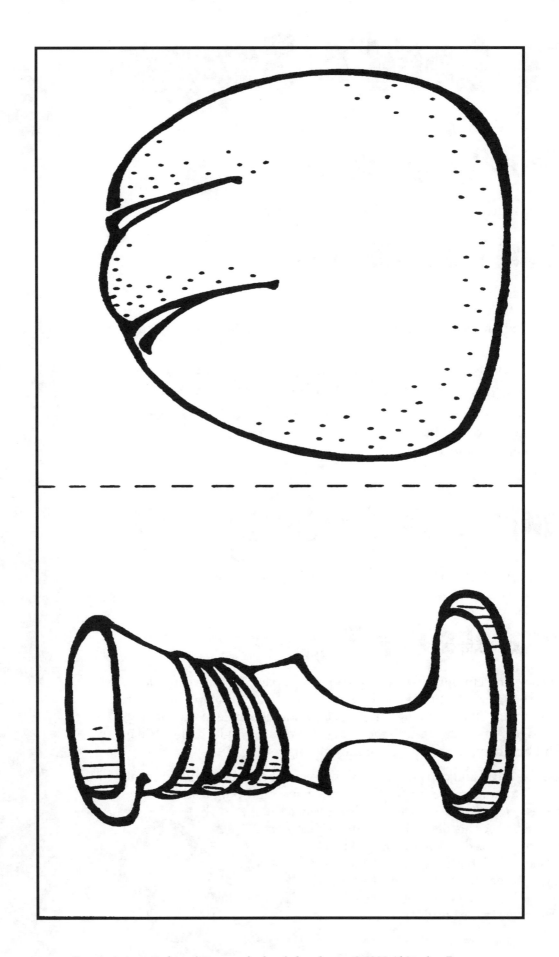

Jesus' Birth

Game 1

Supplies: blindfold

Animal Arias

Have the children be seated and form a circle. Blindfold one player to be IT, and lead him or her to the center of the circle. IT will rotate in place with one arm outstretched. When IT stops, IT will ask the player to whom she or he is pointing to make a sound that baby Jesus might have heard as he slept in the stable. IT must then identify the player from the sound the person makes.

If IT is successful, the player and IT change places. You might want to save this for later in the lesson if you have a class where children don't know each other.

© 1997 Abingdon Press.

Game 2

Supplies: blindfold (optional)

Knock! Knock!

Bring the children together in a circle. The children can sit in chairs or on the floor. Place one chair in the center of the circle.

Say: Whenever we talk about the birth of Jesus, we always talk about how he was born in a stable because there was no room at the inn.

Ask: Who knows what a stable is (*a barn-like place where animals are kept*) What kinds of animals might you find in a stable? (*cows, donkeys, chickens, cats, mice, doves, owls, and so forth*) Let's play a guessing game using these animals. I will pick one of you to be IT. IT will have to listen to the sound of a stable animal and see if IT can decide who is making the sound.

Bible
Luke
2:1-7

73

Select one child to be IT. IT will sit in the chair with his or her eyes closed. You may want to use a blindfold to discourage peeking. Select a child from the circle to be the stable animal. The stable animal will kneel behind IT and knock on the back of the chair.

IT will ask "Who's there?" The child selected will make the sound of an animal that one might have found in the stable at Bethlehem. IT has three opportunities to guess who the child is. If you have a small group, limit the number of guesses to two.

If IT guesses correctly, the animal imitator will take IT's place. If IT fails to guess, the teacher will select another child to make a sound.

Game 3

Supplies: index cards, marker

Story—Go—Round

Say: Today we're hearing about the birth of God's son, Jesus. We hear this story every year at Christmas. We read the story from the Bible. It's a wonderful story to tell over and over again because we love Jesus and know how special he is. But did you ever really think about what it was like to be born in a stable? Close your eyes and imagine what it was like to be in that stable.

Ask: Was it cold or warm in the stable? Was it clean or dirty? How did the stable smell? How did the hay feel? What animals might have been there?

Let the children name all the animals they can think of that might have been in the stable the night that Jesus was born. Write each animal's name down on an index card. Some possible animals might be: sheep, cow, ox, donkey, camel, goat, cat, mouse, spider, flea, or dove. Shuffle the index cards.

Ask: If you had been one of the animals in the stable the night Jesus was born, what would you have seen or thought or done? I am going to roll the ball to someone in the group. Come draw a card with an animal's name on it. Pretend you are that animal and you were present that night. Tell what you saw. Continue around the circle until each of the children has had a chance to share the story from the points of view of the animals.

Ask: Where might Jesus have been born if he were born today? Would it be in a hospital? in a house? Who might be watching?

Say: God didn't send God's Son to enjoy the fine life. God sent Jesus to be raised in the home of ordinary people—people who worked hard for a living. God wanted Jesus to identify with the people he had come to save.

74

Shepherds Come to See Jesus

Game 1

Supplies: sheep tokens (see page 77), pen, scissors, basket or box

Sheep and Shepherd

Make a copy of the sheep tokens (see page 77). Make sure you have enough for each of the children in the class to have one. On the back of two or three put dots or X's. Determine the number of sheep you will need by the number of children you have.

Select one child to be the shepherd. The rest of the children will be sheep. Have them take a sheep token from the basket.

Say: Every shepherd knew just which sheep were his. The sheep knew the sound of the shepherd's voice. Our shepherd here has lost his sheep and is trying to find them. I wonder how he/she will do it?

Say: Each of you is a sheep. Some of you will belong to the shepherd. Some will belong to another shepherd. Our shepherd has to find only the sheep that belong to him or her.

Have the shepherd call out, "Here, sheep." The sheep will all hold their hands up to their mouths. Only the sheep that have a picture with an X or a dot on the back will answer: "Baa, baa." It is up to the shepherd to find all the sheep that belong to his or her herd.

When the shepherd has found all the sheep, select a new shepherd and have the children put their tokens back into the box or basket and draw again.

Say: A shepherd's job was important. But they were not the most powerful or most important in the community. How wonderful that God sent angels to ordinary shepherds to tell the good news of Jesus' birth. We are ordinary people.

Bible
Luke
2:8-20

Talk with the children about the different ways they can tell others about Jesus.

75

© 1997 Abingdon Press.

Game 2

Supplies: Bibles

Wolf! Wolf!

Say: The Bible talks a great deal about shepherds. They were a common sight in Palestine at that time. It was their job to take care of the sheep of the village. One part of the job was to protect the sheep from hungry animals who wanted lamb for dinner. When Jesus grew up, he compared God's love and care to that of the shepherd.

You may want to read some of the Scriptures that refer to shepherds (Psalm 23, Psalm 100, John 10:11, Luke 2:8, Hebrews 13:20).

Say: Let's play a game where we can understand just how hard it was to be a shepherd in Bible times. One of you will be the wolf who is very hungry. One of you will be the shepherd whose job is to protect the sheep from the wolf. The rest of you will be sheep.

Select one child to be the shepherd and one child to be the wolf. The rest of the children will line up behind the shepherd. Each child will hold onto the shoulders of the child in front of him or her.

Say: The wolf wants the juicy lamb at the end of the line. When I say "go," the wolf is going to try to catch the lamb at the end of the line. If the wolf is able to grab onto the waist of the lamb, then the lamb is caught. It is up to all the other sheep and the shepherd to try to protect the lamb without letting go of one another. When the lamb is caught, the wolf takes it back to its den, and the next to the last person becomes the one the wolf is after.

This game is similar to a game played in Turkey called Tilki ve Tavuk (Fox and Hen) and one played in China called Lao Yin Chuo Siao Chi (Eagle and Chickens).

Bring the children back to the circle.

Say: Even though shepherds played an important role in the village, the people did not think very much of them. They were the lowest of the low on the social scale. I wonder why God chose them to be the very first to hear the good news.

77

Simeon and Anna

Game 1

Supplies: flashlight

Who Is It?

Bring the children together in an open area. Select one child to be IT, and have the rest of the children form a line behind her or him.

Say: Simeon and Anna both believed God's promise that a Messiah was coming. They didn't know what the Messiah would look like. All they knew was that they would know this person on sight. Who would have thought that it would be a little tiny baby? Let's play a game and see if we can recognize someone just by a verbal description.

This game is very similar to a game played by the children in Chile called "Who Is It?" The game begins as the child who is IT passes the flashlight over his or her shoulder. The children in the line continue passing it back and forth until IT says, "Stop."

Whoever has the flashlight comes and stands directly behind IT, who is facing away from the group. The group calls out, "Who is it? Who is it? Who is it?"

IT responds by asking three questions, all of which can be answered by a yes or a no. For example, IT may ask, "Is it a boy? Is the person tall? Is the person wearing a green shirt?" Then IT must guess who is standing behind her or him.

If IT guesses correctly, then IT has another turn. If IT guesses incorrectly, another child becomes IT.

Bible
Luke
2:22-38

Game 2

Supplies: chewy candy such as Gummi Bears candies, whistle

Clown Around

Divide the students into three teams. Ask the teams to line up where they can see one another. Give each student three pieces of chewy candy such as Gummi Bears candies. Ask them to hold them until you give them the signal to eat them.

Say: We are going to have a contest. I want you to act like you are clowns and do three things. I will blow the whistle to signal when to begin each one. As you do each one, eat one piece of candy. Use your chewing to help you make expressions. To begin, think about how you would feel if you had been waiting all of your life for something very special to happen. Every day you thought and thought about it and wanted more and more for it to hurry and happen.

Continue: First I want you to chew a piece of candy and show me how you look when you are happy thinking about the special thing that will happen. (*Blow whistle; wait; encourage them to be bouncy and silly.*) Next show me how you feel sad. You are tired of waiting and you are beginning to believe it may never happen. (*Blow whistle; wait; encourage them to be droopy and really sad-looking.*) Now show me how you look when you feel confused and lost. You have waited so long that you don't know what to do next. (*Blow whistle; wait; encourage them to act confused by tripping, falling down, bumping into one another.*)

Praise each team for its creativity. Suggest one way each team excelled. Give them more candies to enjoy eating.

Say: People had waited so long for the Messiah to come. Isaiah prophesied the birth of Jesus almost seven hundred years before Jesus was born. The Bible tells us about two people who had waited all of their lives for the Messiah. They remained faithful and believed he would come. They were especially blessed.

Children in Bible Times

Game

Supplies: small flat stones, old toothbrush, wax paper, acrylic paint, small paintbrushes, film canister and lid

Catch and Toss

Say: Children in Bible times, like children today, had time for games, even though most helped with the chores around the house or in the field. Let's make a game like one the children played long ago in Bible times.

Let the children choose twelve small, relatively flat stones. Using an old toothbrush, remove most of the dirt and dust from each stone. Place the stones on a piece of wax paper. Then let the children decorate their stones with acrylic paint.

Make a container for the stones from a film canister. Paint the outside of the canister and place the stones inside when they are dry.

Say: These stones will be used in a game called "Gap," which is similar to our "Jacks" game. We will use twelve stones, but a child in Bible times would have used twelve small bones from the lamb that was cooked and eaten at the Passover feast. (*If you have access to a butcher and can get the knuckle bones from a lamb, clean and sterilize the bones and let the children handle them.*)

The game is played like this: Children will stretch out their hands, palms down. Have them bring their hands together and hold them together tightly. Have someone place the twelve small stones on the backs of a child's hands. Then the child will lift both hands quickly to toss the stones gently into the air. The child will then turn her or his hands palms-up and see how many stones he or she can catch.

A child may try three times. The child will count the number of stones caught, then pass the stones to the next player.

Bible
Luke
2:41-52

Jesus in the Synagogue

Game 1

Supplies: action cards (see page 83), masking tape, small balls, scissors

No Fair Race!

Make a copy of the action cards (see page 83). Divide the children into two or more teams. (If you have more than eight persons on a team, create another team.) Make a starting line with a strip of masking tape. Then create a masking tape X on the floor about ten feet from the starting line for each team. Place a small ball on each X. Have the children line up behind the starting line.

Say: We are going to have a race. One at a time each player will race down to the X, pick up the ball, and bring it back to the next player in line. That player will race down to the X, place the ball back on it, and come back. The winner will be the team that finishes first. Get ready, get set—oh, I forgot, one team has special instructions.

Have one team draw an action card. Instead of racing down to the ball, the team has to travel using those instructions. For example, instead of running, the team might have to hop on one foot.

Then line up and begin the race. Obviously, the team that can move in a regular fashion will win. Do this again, with the other team drawing an action card. Bring the children to a circle and sit down.

Ask: What was wrong with the race? (*It wasn't fair for one team.*) Why wasn't it fair? (*One team could move normally. The other had special restrictions.*) What would make the race fair? (*If everyone had the same kinds of actions, then it would be fair.*)

Race again. This time have each team have the same restrictions.

Ask: Was it more fun when everyone did the same thing? God sent Jesus to bring good news to all people, regardless of who they were or what their situation. Some people were glad to hear this. Others were not.

Bible
Luke
4:16-22

Game 2

Supplies: clean kitchen sponges

De—do—wop Boppers

Say: It isn't easy to get the good news out today—and in Jesus' time this was even harder. One thing made it even more difficult. The people who were present when Jesus announced his relationship to God were people whom Jesus had known all of his life. They were his neighbors from when he was a boy. They were friends of his mother, and they were people who had come to Joseph to get things built. And then in the story Jesus said something that was totally inexcusable.

Ask: Have you ever had that happen to you where people who know you don't think you can possibly be anything special?

Say: Let's play a game. I want you to get into pairs. One of you will be Partner A. The other will be Partner B. Sit on the floor facing each other with your feet extended straight out in front of you. Partner A's feet will be up against Partner B's feet. Partner A will tell something about him or herself. It can be true, or it can be made up. If Partner B thinks it is true, Partner B will say "I believe it." Partner B will throw the sponge at Partner A if he or she thinks the statement is false. (*Even though it is soft and would not hurt, caution the children about aiming the sponge at one another's faces.*) If Partner B throws the sponge and the statement happens to be true, he or she will hand over the sponge, and it will be Partner A's turn to listen.

Play for several minutes, encouraging the children to come up with some things about themselves that no one would know. When it looks like everyone has had a chance, collect the sponges and bring the children back to the circle.

Ask: What did you learn? (*There are many things about each other that are unfamiliar.*) Do you think that same sort of thing happened to Jesus? Did people learn something about him that they hadn't known before?

© 1999 Abingdon Press.

Walk backwards	Walk on tiptoe
Crawl	Hop on one foot
Walk with your eyes closed	Take baby steps
Walk heel to toe	Do a crab walk

Centurion's Servant

Game

Supplies: rescue cards (see page 85), scissors, paper bag

9—1—1 Rescue!

Have all but one of the students sit in chairs in a large circle. Leave enough space between the chairs that the players can move freely between them. Ask the remaining player to stand in the middle of the circle.

Say: (*Name*) will be the doctor.

Photocopy three sets of the rescue cards (see page 85) and cut them apart. Put two sets of cards in a paper bag and give the bag to the doctor. Give each of the players who are sitting one of the cards from the remaining set, except for the 911 card. (If you have a large group, photocopy extra cards. If you have a small group, give each player more than one card.)

Say: These are things we may need if we are sick or injured. These are also things we can give or ask for when someone needs our help.

Ask the doctor to shake the bag to scramble the cards.

Say: The doctor is going to take two cards out of the bag and call out what they are: ambulance, blanket, first aid kit, glass of water, wheelchair, stretcher, hot soup, and thermometer. Any players holding those cards must jump up and quickly exchange seats. If the doctor pulls out a 911 card, (*Hold up the extra card from the set to show everyone and then put it in the bag.*) then everyone jumps up and changes seats. The doctor can try to get one of the empty seats. Anyone who is still standing becomes the new doctor.

© 1998 Abingdon Press.

Bible
Luke
7:1-10

Two by Two

Game 1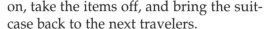

Supplies: two old suitcases or gym bags; old clothes such as a large sweatshirt, sweatpants, pair of large sneakers, hat, scarf, pair of gloves; masking tape

Pack It Up!

Fill two old suitcases or gym bags with old clothes. Each bag will need a similar set of items, such as a large sweatshirt, a pair of sweatpants, a pair of large sneakers, a hat, a scarf, and a pair of gloves. Check with parents of the children in your class, or visit a local thrift store and then donate the clothing back to the clothes closet. Make sure the items of clothing are clean.

Divide the children into two teams. Have them stand in a line one behind the other. Mark a line with masking tape about ten feet from the group. Then give one suitcase to the leader of each team.

Ask: When you go on a trip, and you will be away from home for several days, what are some things you take with you?

Let the children share items they would pack.

Say: Jesus' friends were sent out on a trip too. They would be gone for many days. But what they took with them was a great deal less than most of you take. Let's play a packing game. Each team will be given a suitcase of clothing. Every person on the team will get to put the items on, take the items off, and bring the suitcase back to the next travelers.

At the starting signal, the first person on each team must carry the suitcase to the finish line, open it, dump out the contents, put on each of the items of clothing, take off the items of clothing, repack the suitcase, close the suitcase, and run back to the starting line. The game continues until all members of one team have finished.

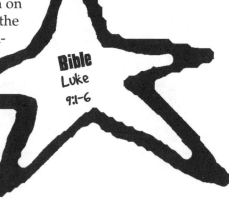

Bible
Luke
9:1-6

86

If you have a child in your class with mobility problems, try to make the items of clothing those that the child can put on or take off relatively easily.

Game 2

Supplies: inflatable beach ball

Get the Message!

Ask: What did Jesus tell his disciples to do on their journey? (*Tell everyone the good news, heal the sick, raise the dead, proclaim God's power.*) What were the disciples supposed to take with them on their journey? (*only the clothes they were now wearing*) What couldn't they take? (*extra clothing or sandals, a walking stick or food*) How would they get fed? (*The people of the villages would care for them.*) What were they to do if the people would not provide for them? (*just be on their way*)

Say: Jesus wanted the disciples to travel together and to work together to spread the good news about God's kingdom. Let's play a game where each of you has to work with another person to get the message to the next.

Have the children form two lines, standing side by side. Divide the children into pairs. Then divide the pairs into two groups. Have one set of pairs at one end of the room and the other set of pairs at the other end of the room.

Place the inflatable beach ball between the first pair of children. That pair is to make its way across the room to the other set of pairs, who will receive the beach ball and return it in the very same way to the next group.

Play until each pair has had a chance to take the beach ball to the next group. If you have a small group, you may want to play several times.

The Good Samaritan

Game 1

Supplies: masking tape, shoeboxes

Do the Jericho Jog

Set a beginning and ending line with masking tape. Tell the children that one end is Jericho and the other end is Jerusalem. Remove the top of the shoeboxes. Set the two boxes on the floor.

Say: The Jericho road is a dangerous road. Many thieves and robbers hid in the rocks along the road to attack unsuspecting travelers. Let's see if each of you can make it to the other end of the road without being attacked.

Have one child be the caller. The other children will be travelers. One half will line up at Jerusalem. The other half will line up at Jericho. The first child in line at Jerusalem will step into the shoeboxes, one foot in each box. When you say "Go!" that child will step along the Jericho road, keeping his or her feet in the shoeboxes. If he or she makes it to the other end, he steps out of the shoeboxes, and another child steps in them and tries to make it to Jerusalem.

Say: The object is to get to Jericho from Jerusalem or to get to Jerusalem from Jericho. If the caller shouts out, "Robbers and thieves," the traveler has to the count of ten to get either back to where he or she came from, or to get to the next city. If the traveler can't make it to either spot, he sits on the side of the road until another traveler tags him or her.

Game 2

Supplies: clothespins, sponges, paper cups, crayons, masking tape

Over the Edge

The object of this game is to work together to accomplish a certain task. Establish with masking tape a beginning and ending line at opposite ends of the playing area.

Bible
Luke
10:29-37

Set a table at the ending line. On the table place these items: clothespins, sponges, paper cups, and crayons. Divide the children into pairs. Let them decide who will be the balancer and who will be the supporter.

Say: When I say "go," the teams will go to the table, balance one item on the balancer's head, and come back to the starting line. The balancer and supporter will change places. Then the teams will go to the table, balance two items on the balancer's head or shoulders, and come back. This continues until the teams complete five items. The first team to get five items wins. If an item falls off the balancer's head or shoulder, then it is up to the support person to put it back on.

This game will show the children how important it is to help one another.

Game 3

Supplies: skein of yarn, scissors

Who's My Neighbor?

Bring the children together in a circle. Roll a skein of yarn into a ball of yarn.

Say: Even though the priest and the Levite were technically neighbors to the man who was injured, they did not stop to help. I'm sure they had good reasons, but they still did not help. The Samaritan who technically was a foreigner in this part of the world, and not a neighbor in the known sense of the word, did stop and help.

Ask: Who was the good neighbor? (*the Samaritan*) I am going to hold this ball of yarn. You are going to ask me, "Who is your neighbor?" I will name someone and toss the ball to him or her, continuing to hold onto a part of the yarn. The group will ask the person I threw it to: "Who is your neighbor?" That person will name someone and toss the ball to him or her, continuing to hold onto a part of the yarn. We will continue until everyone is holding onto a part of the yarn.

Let everyone get connected.

Say: We are all neighbors, even though we do not live next door to each other or even on the same street. We are neighbors with persons who live in our city, our state, our country. We are neighbors with persons who live in this country or in countries far away. God knows that we needed to learn to care about our neighbors, no matter where they are.

As you reroll the yarn, cut small portions of the yarn (about six inches long) and tie them around each child's wrist as a reminder to be a good neighbor.

The Ten Lepers

Game 1

Supplies: inflatable beach ball

Unclean! Unclean!

Say: Today we're hearing about some men who had a serious skin disease called leprosy. People who had leprosy not only had to wear special clothes that set them apart, but they also had to live apart from the rest of the community. If they did have an opportunity to come into town, wherever they went they had to shout, "Unclean, unclean!" so that people would know they were coming and would avoid them.

Ask: How would you like to live like that? Do you think it would be fun? How would you feel if everyone started running away when you got close? Let's play a game where some of you will be the townsfolk and the rest of you will be the ones saying, "Unclean, unclean."

This game should be played in a very open area. If the weather is good, take the children outside. Give one player the inflatable beachball.

Say: No one wants to be touched by Unclean Jean, or have anything that Unclean Jean has touch them. When Unclean Jean tosses the ball into the air, you may scatter about the playing area. But when Unclean Jean catches the ball and shouts, "Stop!" everyone must freeze in place. Unclean Jean may then take three steps in any direction and throw the ball at any player. (*The rule is you may only throw the ball waist level or below.*) Players may dodge, stoop, or swivel to get out of the way, but one foot must remain in place. If you are tagged by the ball, then you too are "unclean" and must come to the center.

When Unclean Jean has taken his or her shot with the ball, then the group comes back to the circle, and it begins again. Any player who is now "unclean" has an opportunity to take three steps in any direction and try to tag someone else during the next turn.

Say: I am sure that a person would not want to live that way and would be very grateful if something happened to cure him or her. But this wasn't exactly what happened.

Bible
Luke
17:11-19

90

Game 2

Supplies: blindfold

Who Said Thanks?

Ask: Why do you think nine of the men forgot to say thank you? (*Perhaps they were excited to be healed. Maybe they didn't realize that it was Jesus who healed them.*) Have you ever forgotten to say thank you to someone? Has anyone ever forgotten to say thank you to you? How did you feel? Why is it important to say thank you? (*to let a person know that you appreciate what he or she has done for you*)

Say: Saying thank you is a way to show other people that we like what they have done. Out of the ten men that Jesus healed, only one came back to say thank you. Do you think it made Jesus sad? Let's play a game to see if you can tell who says thank you.

Have the children form a circle with their chairs. Put one chair in the center of the circle. Select one child from the group. Have him or her sit in the middle chair. Blindfold that child.

Say: I will choose someone to come up behind you and say, "Thank you." That person can try to disguise his or her voice. Listen carefully and see if you can tell who it is. If you guess who it is, then you change places. If you can't guess, then you get to try again.

Play until everyone has a chance to say thank you.

Zacchaeus

Game 1

Supplies: coins

Downright Upright!

Ask: What did Zacchaeus do that was dishonest? (*He took more tax money than was required*.) Is it dishonest to collect taxes? (*No, but it is dishonest to take more than the prescribed amount*.) What did Zacchaeus do to make amends? (*He gave half of his possessions to the poor and returned more than four times the money he had stolen*.)

Say: Zacchaeus was a thief. But when Jesus came into his life, Zacchaeus decided to change his ways. Jesus knew that God sent him into the world to find those people who were doing wrong and bring them back to the right path.

Have the children form a circle with their hands behind their backs. Select one child to be IT.

Say: Jesus could look into Zacchaeus' heart. Jesus knew that Zacchaeus had done wrong but that he basically wasn't a bad person; he was just a man who had strayed from the right path. Sometimes we can tell when someone isn't telling the truth. I am going to go around the circle and place "stolen" coins in your hands—some of you, that is. (*To make the process a little easier, identify how many coins you are going to pass out*.) IT will go around the circle and ask each of you: "Do you have my money?" Each person is to respond: "No, I'm downright upright!" If IT thinks you have one of the stolen coins, then IT will tap you on the shoulder. Hold out your hands in front. If you have a coin, then you come to the center. If you don't, you stay where you are. IT can make three wrong guesses; then we'll start the game all over again.

Play until several of the children have an opportunity to be IT or until the children begin to lose interest.

Ask: Was it easy or hard to see who was being honest when you were being IT? Was it easy or hard to be dishonest when you were in the circle?

Bible
Luke
19:1–10

Say: It's hard not to tell the truth, because we know how important it is to be honest. Even in a game, we know that being honest is important.

Game 2

Honest to Goodness

Say: The Bible teaches us to be honest. Zacchaeus was a dishonest man. He took money that did not belong to him. The people he stole from could ill afford to lose the money. Zacchaeus was not doing good to others. But there is more to being honest than just not stealing. Being honest also means to tell the truth, to be fair, to mean what you say, and to be upright and trustworthy.

Ask: Can you think of a time when someone has not been honest with you? (*Invite the children to share events in their lives.*) What did you do when you found out? How did you feel about that person then?

Say: I am going to make a statement. If the person is being honest, give a cheer. If the person is not being honest, put your head in your hands and say, "Oh, no!"

Use these statements:

Darryl cheated on his math test so he would get a passing grade.
Amy told her father that she was the one who broke the window.
Elizabeth told her mother that her jacket was stolen when she really left it on the school bus.
When no one was looking, Jeremy moved his game piece so he'd be closer to the finish.
When Melanie's best friend asked her if she liked her new backpack, Melanie answered, "It's so like you. You really like those colors!" But Melanie didn't personally like the colors herself.
Kyle admitted that he forgot to walk the dog and offered to clean up the mess in the kitchen.

Bring the children together in a prayer circle.

Pray: Dear God, help us always to be honest. When we are honest, we show other people that we love you. Amen.

Jesus, God's Son

Game 1

Pass the Word

Invite the children to sit down on the floor in a circle. Sit cross-legged so that each child's knees are touching (or nearly touching).

Say: Jesus is God's son. Pass it on.

As you say the sentence, make a special motion with your hands, such as clapping, snapping, patting your legs, wiggling your fingers, and so forth. The next child in the circle will say the same sentence, repeat your hand motion, and add an additional hand motion of his or her own.

This will continue around the circle until there is a great deal of hand jive going on.

When the statement and the motion come full circle, let the child to your right make a statement and start a hand motion going in the opposite direction around the circle. Play long enough for several children to make statements about what they know about Jesus.

Say: Jesus tells his friends that they are to pass on his word and make disciples of all people.

Bible
John
1:32-34

Game 2

Play a Name Game

Bring the children together in a circle.

Say: Names are very important. Names tell us who we are. Names help us talk to one another. If each of you didn't have a name, I might have to say "Hey, you, with the red shirt. Pick up that book, please." And if everyone was named George or Beverly, no one would know who I was talking to if I just said, "George, get the crayons out." So names are very special. Since names are such helpful things, let's play a game using our names.

Begin this clapping rhythm: Pat knees with both hands. Clap hands together. Snap the fingers of the right hand. Snap the fingers of the left hand. Repeat until the children are all in rhythm.

Say: I will say the verse and then call on a person in this circle. Then that person says the verse and calls on a person. This all sounds very easy, except that we have to stay in rhythm as we call on one another.

The verse is as follows:

Let's play a game
Using all our names.
I'm thinking of a person,
And the name is (*name of child*).

Try this several times until the children get the hang of it. This is also a good game to get the children acquainted with one another and settled down before beginning another activity. Make sure every child gets an opportunity to respond to the verse.

Ask: Who is the Son of God? (*Jesus*)

Road to Emmaus

Game 1

Supplies: blindfold

Who Is It?

Invite the children to form a circle on the floor. Put a chair in the center of the circle. Select one child to be IT.

Say: Today we're hearing about a time when Jesus' friends don't recognize him at first. Let's see if you can identify one another. The only catch is, the person in the chair will be blindfolded. The only way he or she can "see" a person is by touching his or her face.

Have IT sit in the chair. Blindfold him or her. Then point to a child and have him or her come up and kneel in front of IT. IT will touch that person's face and try to figure out who it is. Make sure every child has a chance to be IT or to be one of the children whose identity IT is trying to guess.

Game 2

Supplies: brown paper grocery sack, items of clothing (hat, scarf, sweatshirt, sweatpants, shoes

Pack It Up!

Say: Today we're talking about a special journey down the road from Jerusalem to Emmaus. But the men never made it to their destination—they turned around and came back with excellent news. Jesus was alive! Let's pretend we are taking a journey. Like in Bible times, we won't carry suitcases. People at that time carried all their belongings in baskets or bags. We will get to our destination, dress, undress, repack the bag, and return to our original starting place.

Bible
Luke
24:13–31

96

Divide the children into teams. You will need no more than four persons on a team. Pack a brown paper grocery sack for each team of four. Use these items of clothing: hat, scarf, sweatshirt, sweatpants, shoes.

Give each team leader one of the bags. At the starting signal the first person on the team will carry the bag to the finish line, open it up, dump out the contents, put on all the clothing items, come back to the starting line, take off all the clothes, and put them in the bag for the second person in line.

The game will continue until all members of each team have finished. If you have a small class, let them work against time rather than each other.

Game 3

Supplies: blindfold

Excuse Me, Please!

Ask: Where were the men going when they met the stranger on the road? (*Emmaus*) What made the stranger angry? (*They still had problems believing what Jesus had told them.*) When did the men recognize Jesus? (*when he broke the bread at mealtime*) What did they do then? (*They rushed back to Jerusalem to tell the others.*) Why didn't they recognize Jesus at first? (*The Bible doesn't tell us.*)

Say: Perhaps they were not expecting to see Jesus, a man who had been dead and resurrected. Perhaps they were not very familiar with him and just didn't recognize him. The Bible leaves this as a mystery to us. Let's see if you can be more observant.

Have the children come together in the open area of the room. Select one child to be IT. Put a blindfold on IT.

Say: Everyone will be able to move freely about the room until IT says, "Stop!" Then everyone has to stop moving. IT will move about and try to find someone. Whenever IT touches someone, IT will say "Excuse me, please. But who are you?" Then IT will try to discover who that person is by feeling his or her face and head. If IT makes a correct identification, that person will become the next IT, and the game will begin again.

Play until all the children have had a chance to be IT or until the children get bored. Make sure for safety's sake that there are no obstacles for IT to trip over while blindfolded.

Say: The men may not have recognized Jesus at first; but once they did, they hurried back to Jerusalem to spread the good news. Jesus is alive!

The Woman at the Well

Game

Supplies: well (see page 100), two bowls, water, two empty jars, plastic garbage bags or a plastic drop cloth, plastic spoons, towels, measuring cup, whistle

Splish Splash Relay

Set up the relay. You will need: two tables, about ten feet apart, two bowls of water, and two empty jars. Cover the floor between the two tables with plastic garbage bags or a plastic drop cloth.

Divide the children into two or three teams. Give each child a plastic spoon.

Make two copies of the well (see page 100). Place the bowls of water inside the well. Have the children line up behind the table with the empty jars. Cover the tables with towels or a plastic drop cloth to catch any spillover.

Say: Water is very important to us. We use water every day. We drink it, we cook with it, we bathe in it. We even play in it. In Bible times, water was not so easy to get. People had to make a trip to the village well to get water. They did not have running water in their homes.

Say: One of the most important jobs a woman did in Bible times was going to the well to get the water for the family, in addition to all her other jobs. The woman usually made the trip early in the morning and then again just before the evening.

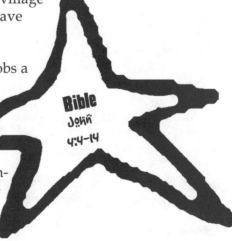

Bible
John
4:4-14

Say: We are going to go to the well and get water and bring it back to our families. The only problem is that the water has to be carried in a spoon.

Continue: When I blow the whistle, I want the first player to take the team's spoon and race to the well, scoop up a spoonful of water, and race back to her or his team jar. Empty the spoon into the team jar and pass the spoon to the next person in the line. Be careful—the faster you go, the more water you spill, and the more trips you will have to make. When I blow the whistle again, the team with the most water in its jar is the champion.

Have the children walk only on the plastic drop cloth as they get their water and bring it back to the family. Use a measuring cup to determine which team has the most water.

Make sure everyone has had a chance to carry water at least twice before blowing the whistle to end the relay.

Say: The people in Bible times took great pride in the work they did. They did everything to the glory of God.

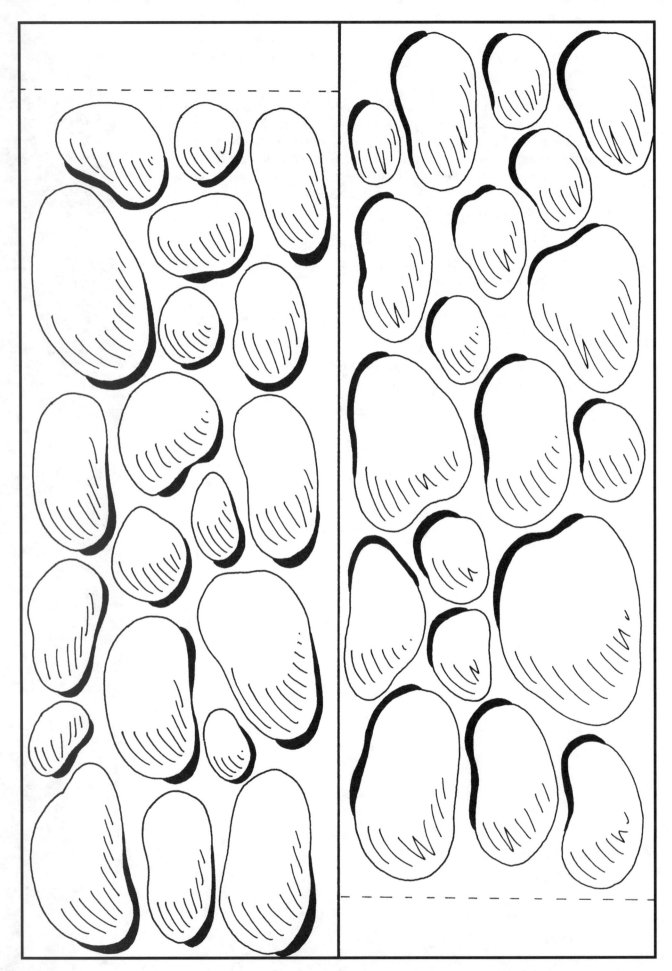

Palm Sunday

Game 1

Supplies: cloak pattern (see page 103), crayons or felt-tip markers, whistle

Oodles of Cloaks

Greet the children as they arrive. Give each child a copy of the cloak pattern (see page 103). Have the children use crayons or felt-tip markers to decorate the cloak in any way they choose.

Say: In Bible times people wore cloaks that looked similar to this. The cloaks kept them warm when it was cold. It was their blanket when they slept outside. It was a very important piece of clothing. In fact, sometimes a person would use his cloak as a temporary payment for a debt.

Divide the children into teams of two. Assign one child to be Player A and one child to be Player B. Player A will be in charge of designating the path. Player B will be in charge of walking.

Say: Jesus made a special journey to the city of Jerusalem. The people who heard he was coming rushed out to greet him. They waved palm branches, and they put their cloaks on the road for the donkey to walk on. What a strange thing to do! Let's pretend we are Jesus and his donkey. We are going to make the trip to Jerusalem, and we can walk only across the cloaks. Let's see how long it will take us to make the trip. When I blow the whistle, everyone begins. When I blow the whistle a second time, everyone will stop.

Have Player A place one of the cloaks on the floor. Player B will step on it. Then Player A will place the second cloak on the floor, and Player B will step on it. Player A will remove the first cloak and place it on the floor in front of Player B, and so on until the teams reach Jerusalem.

Say: Jesus must have been very important for persons to use their cloaks in such a way.

© 1998 Abingdon Press.

Bible
John
12:12-16

101

Game 2

Supplies: peanuts, basket or bowl, paper towels

Found a Peanut

Have each child reach into the basket or bowl and draw out a peanut in a shell.

Say: I want you to take this peanut back to your seat and study it very carefully. I want you to know it so well that you can pick it out among all the other peanuts.

Tell the children not to eat the peanut until after the activity is over.

Collect all the peanuts back in the bowl. Then spread them out on a table on paper towels. Let each child go to the stack of peanuts and find his or her particular peanut.

If you have a very large group (over ten children), do this in groups to prevent mix-ups.

Ask: How did you know it was your peanut? (*Let the children share their criteria for identification.*)

Say: We are going to talk about a special way of remembering Jesus, a way our church uses during worship. Now you can eat your peanuts. (*Note: Be careful to first find out if any of the children may have allergies to peanuts.*)

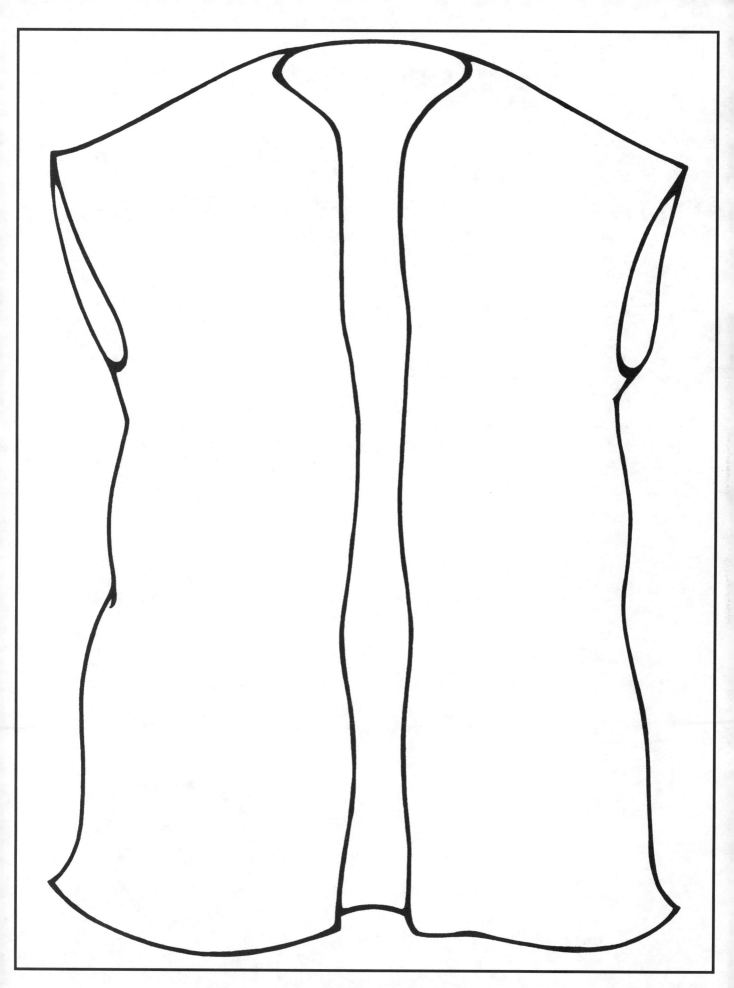

Easter

Game 1

Get to the Garden

Bring the children to an open area of the room. Create a starting line on one side of the room and a safety zone on the other side. Have the children line up on the starting line.

Say: The safety zone is the garden. That is the place where everyone wants to be.

Say: On the morning after the sabbath, Mary Magdalene and the other Mary hurried to the garden. They wanted to give their friend Jesus a proper burial. Showing respect to a man who was considered a criminal was probably not the smartest thing they could do. So they came just as the sun was coming up, before there was anyone around. Surely the guards would have no trouble with two women coming to minister to their friend. Let's see if we can get into the garden without disturbing the guards.

Select one child to be IT. IT will stand guarding the garden. When IT gives the signal, all the children will try to sneak to the garden. When IT turns around, anyone IT catches moving becomes the next Roman guard. Play until several children have had an opportunity to be IT.

Say: The religious officials had heard Jesus' statement that on the third day God would raise him from the dead. They didn't believe it, but they wanted to make sure the disciples didn't sneak in, steal the body, and then claim Jesus had risen. That's why they stationed guards at the tomb. Weren't they surprised to find out that they couldn't thwart God's plans!

Bible
John
20:1-10

Game 2

High—Five Hand Jive

Have the children form a large circle. Make sure there is space to move without running into anything. The children will stand facing the center with their hands behind them, palms up.

Say: When Mary came to the tomb that morning, she got a big surprise. She came in sadness, ready to prepare Jesus' body for burial. But instead, she found an angel who told her that Jesus was alive. Then she came face-to-face with Jesus himself. What happiness! What joy! Mary couldn't keep the news to herself—she had to hurry to tell the others. So she ran all the way. We too, as followers of Jesus, can share the joy of Jesus' resurrection with others.

Continue: Let's play a game. I want you to pretend that you are all Jesus' disciples. I will select one of you to be the one who found the empty tomb. That person will walk around the outside of the circle and slap the hands of one of the disciples. The two will then run in opposite directions, racing for the vacant spot. Upon meeting at the other side of the circle, they stop, and the first person will say, "Jesus is alive!" and the other person will respond, "Hallelujah!" Then they will both give a High-Five Hand Jive.

The High-Five Hand Jive is done as follows:

Hit right hands together.
Hit left hands together.
Hit both hands together.
First player holds hands in front of body, palms up, and second player slaps them.
Second player holds hands in front of body, palms up, and first player hits them.
Bump right hips twice.
Bump left hips twice.

When this ritual is complete, then both players will continue on around the circle, racing for the vacant place. The first one there will get to keep the place. The second person will become IT and begin walking around the circle. Players will be eliminated who fail to stop and say, "Jesus is risen!" and "Hallelujah!" and do the High-Five Hand Jive.

Lydia

Game 1

Supplies: obstacles (see page 107), scissors, paper, ping-pong balls, masking tape

Spread the Good News

Create a start and a finish line at both ends of the table with masking tape. Photocopy the obstacles (see page 107). Cut them apart; fold them on the dotted lines. Attach the wicket shapes around the table, creating an obstacle course. Place the wickets so the children can progress down the table, but not in a straight line. Tape the bases to the table. Make each wicket high enough to allow a ping-pong ball to pass easily.

Give each child a piece of paper. Have him or her fold the paper accordion-style to form a fan. The children will blow the ball with the fan. Each ball must go through all the wickets and cross the finish line. A ball that blows off the table may be put at the place where it blew off. For a large class, make several tables. The children may play in groups of two to four.

> **Say:** Try to get the good news ball from one end of the table to the other. Go through each obstacle, but don't touch the ball with your hands. You must move the ball with a fan. If the ball blows off the table, set it back on the table where it blew off and continue.

© 1997 Abingdon Press.

Game 2

Good News Gossip

Have the children sit in a circle. Play a game of good news gossip. Begin a statement about Jesus. Let the children whisper the statement to the person next to them. That person will whisper it to the person next to them. Once you have told the statement, you can't repeat it.

Use statements such as: "Jesus was born in Bethlehem," "Jesus said to love one another," and "Jesus is God's only Son. Remind the children to pass the message on as correctly as possible. You only have one chance.

106

© 1997 Abingdon Press.

Bible
Acts
16:11-15

People who don't know Jesus.

People who don't want to be different.

People who live far away.

People who don't want to change.

People who need to see to believe.

People who are set in their ways.

People who live across the ocean.

People who are afraid.

People who

Working for Christ

Game

Supplies: plastic garbage bags, newspapers

No Hands Allowed

Say: God calls us every day to do special things to help people. Sometimes helping others is easy; sometimes it's not. Let's play a game of helping.

Have the children stuff the garbage bags with newspapers. Tie them securely. The object of this game is for teams to see how many garbage bags they can carry without using their hands.

Set the garbage bags around the room. Divide the children into teams of five to six children. If you have a small class, the whole class will be a team. Begin with two children holding both hands.

Say: Let's see how many garbage bags each team can carry at one time. You have five minutes. You have to pick up each bag without using your hands. When you need another person to help, just yell "Help!" Another team member can come and join the circle.

Say: Sometimes jobs are just too hard to do by yourself. Sometimes you can use a little help to get things done. We can always ask for help. We can also remember that God is there to help us.

Bible
I Corinthians
3:9

Love One Another

Game 1

Twitch, Shake, Wiggle

Say: Today's Bible verse says that we are to love, not in word or speech, but in truth and action. Let's play a game where we do not use a word, but use an action instead.

Bring everyone together in a circle. The first player begins by saying, "The baby went to sleep." The rest of the group answers, "How did the baby go to sleep?" The first player then says, "The baby went to sleep like this, like this," repeating a small gesture such as nodding the head or twisting the wrist. The rest of the group mimics the gesture and answers, "Like this, like this."

The entire group continues to repeat the gesture as the next player in line says, "The baby went to sleep," and the others respond as before. The second player adds another gesture to the first, so that now there are two movements to keep going. The game continues around the circle, each player adding a gesture. By the end of the game, the entire group should be twitching, wiggling and shaking all over the place.

Ask: What do you think it means that God wants us to love in truth and action, not in word and speech? (*It's more important to do something than to talk about doing something and not doing it.*)

Say: I am going to give you a setting and what happened. You decide whether it is words (*Yakkety Yak*) or actions. (*Zoom*)

"I promise to do my homework first," said Zack. But Zack watched television instead. (*Yakkety Yak*)

"I won't ride my bicycle in the street anymore," said Jill. Jill kept her bike on the sidewalk until she was a better rider. (*Zoom*)

"I'll put a quarter of my allowance each week in the mission offering," said Alexander. But on Sunday he had already spent his allowance. (*Yakkety Yak*)

"I'll help clean the garage on Saturday," promised Megan. But she forgot that her soccer team was having a picnic in the park. (*Yakkety Yak*)

"I'll read you a story after supper," said Willie.
   After helping his mother clear the table, Willie read his little brother a story. (*Zoom*)

Bible
I John
3:18

Game 2

Supplies: ball

Who Do You Love?

Bring the children together in a circle. They can sit on the floor or sit in chairs.

Say: Let's play a game called "Who Do You Love?" I will have someone begin by tossing the ball to him or her. That person will describe someone in the group that she or he loves. When the person who is being described recognizes himself or herself, that person jumps up and says, "That's me!" If that child is correct, the person doing the describing tosses the ball to the child who answered correctly, and she or he becomes the describer.

Toss the ball to one of the children.

Ask: Who do you love?

Play until every child has a turn or until the children begin to lose interest.

© 1998 Abingdon Press.

Game 3

Supplies: blindfold

Who's My Neighbor?

Say: Not only did Jesus tell us that we should love God with our whole hearts and minds, but he also said that we should love our neighbors as ourselves. But who are our neighbors? Let's play a game and see if we can find out for ourselves.

Select one person to be IT. IT is blindfolded and stands in the center. When IT says "Go," all the children switch places. When IT says, "Stop!" the children freeze immediately. IT then points in any direction. The person pointed to comes forward and stands in front of IT. IT says "Howdy, neighbor." The player who is standing in front of IT must say, "Howdy." This can be repeated three times only. If IT guesses the player's identity, then the two change places. If the guess is wrong, the person picked returns to the circle, and the one who is IT selects a new player.

Say: It's fun to be good neighbors.

110

© 1998 Abingdon Press.

Index by Bible Reference

Index by Subject